MEREDITH®BOOKS ● DES MOINES, IOWA

HGTV The Best of Designers' Challenge

Editor: Amy Tincher-Durik
Writer and Project Editor: Amber Barz
Art Director: The Design Office of Jerry J. Rank
Copy Chief: Terri Fredrickson
Publishing Operations Manager: Karen Schirm
Edit and Design Production Coordinator: Mary Lee Gavin
Editorial Assistants: Kaye Chabot, Kairee Windsor
Marketing Product Managers: Aparna Pande, Isaac Petersen, Gina Rickert, Stephen Rogers,
    Brent Wiersma, Tyler Woods
Book Production Managers: Pam Kvitne, Marjorie J. Schenkelberg, Rick von Holdt, Mark Weaver
Contributing Copy Editor: Amanda Knief
Contributing Proofreaders: Carol Boker, Dan Degen, Beth Havey
Cover Photographer: Edmund Barr
Contributing Photographers: Edmund Barr, Gordon Beall, Dick Dickinson, Beth Singer
Indexer: Kathleen Poole

Meredith® Books

Executive Director, Editorial: Gregory H. Kayko
Executive Director, Design: Matt Strelecki
Senior Editor/Group Manager: Vicki Ingham
Senior Associate Design Director: Mick Schnepf

Publisher and Editor in Chief: James D. Blume
Editorial Director: Linda Raglan Cunningham
Executive Director, Marketing: Jeffrey B. Myers
Executive Director, New Business Development: Todd M. Davis
Executive Director, Sales: Ken Zagor
Director, Operations: George A. Susral
Director, Production: Douglas M. Johnston
Business Director: Jim Leonard

Vice President and General Manager: Douglas J. Guendel

Meredith Publishing Group

President: Jack Griffin
Senior Vice President: Bob Mate

Meredith Corporation

Chairman and Chief Executive Officer: William T. Kerr
President and Chief Operating Officer: Stephen M. Lacy

In Memoriam: E.T. Meredith III (1933–2003)

designers'**challenge**

1 ROOM 3 WAYS

designers'challenge table of contents

1 ROOM
3 WAYS

designers'challenge innovativesolutionsfor

HGTV's *Designers' Challenge* show follows homeowners through the exhilarating decision-making process of selecting from three designers' room renovation plans to solve a "problem" space. In the end only one design is implemented, and viewers watch as the new vision springs to life. If you are a fan of *Designers' Challenge*, this is your opportunity to relive the fun of your favorite episodes and

problemspaces

linger a little longer in these fabulous spaces. Or perhaps you are looking for ideas to transform your home to make it more beautiful and livable—or maybe you are planning to build a new home and you want design ideas that will truly make your house a dream home. Whatever your goal is, this book won't disappoint!

HGTV The Best of Designers' Challenge Problem Rooms Solved Three Ways brings you the excitement of the program by highlighting 18 completed rooms—including kitchens, living rooms, dining rooms, home offices, bedrooms, and baths—with beautiful photos and the options featured on the show. Similar to the show, you will find:

THE CHALLENGE THE HOMEOWNER PRESENTED to the designers, including the allotted budget.

THE SOLUTION EACH DESIGNER PRESENTED to the homeowner by way of colorful drawings, fabrics swatches, and/or floor plans.

THE DESIGN ULTIMATELY CHOSEN by the homeowner.

COLOR PHOTOGRAPHS OF THE COMPLETED SPACE, along with advice on how to get the look in your own home as well as the total materials and labor costs of the completed project.

AND MUCH MORE. This book goes beyond the parameters of the 30-minute show to provide you with insight into giving a room a fresh new look with surface treatments (such as paint on the walls or new flooring) and rearranging the existing furnishings. Major remodeling projects, including to-the-studs kitchen and bath renovations, offer solutions for turning the least-liked room in your home into your family's favorite gathering space or your very own personal retreat. Whether you are planning a big-budget remodeling or a bit of furniture refurbishing, you'll find valuable budgeting information—including how to get high-end looks for less—remodeling survival tips, and fail-safe design principles. As an added bonus, the designers featured on the show give you valuable insight into their design philosophies, which will both help you make smart decisions if you plan to tackle your home redo yourself and give you tools for selecting a professional to do the work for you.

FOR YOUR READING EASE the book is divided into three sections: "Changes on the Surface," "Remake by Remodeling," and "Smart Selections."

changes on the **surface**

When the size and the features of any given room are just right, but the space isn't functioning the way you want it to or it just needs a new look, it's time to refresh! The rooms included in this section get a boost in style from new furnishings, new arrangements, and new colors. Innovative yet easy-to-achieve surface updates, such as refacing a fireplace and installing new flooring, are also included.

remake by remodeling

To achieve utmost style and function, some rooms need to be altered beyond surface treatments: cabinets added or removed, windows and doors installed, walls torn down. Besides highlighting great remodeled spaces, this section also includes special topics you should consider when planning a remodel, such as ensuring the finished space "fits" the existing style and architecture of your home.

smart selections

Now that you've seen the possibilities, it's time to plan your dream makeover. This section provides up-to-date information on the elements and surfaces that make a room: appliances, cabinetry, countertops, flooring, lighting, windows, doors, and moldings. Additionally you'll learn how to select and collaborate with interior designers, contractors, and builders to ensure project success.

Are you thinking about embarking on a decorating or remodeling journey, or do you just enjoy looking at gorgeous, well-designed homes from across America? Either way, we are happy you've taken this opportunity to view beautifully appointed rooms as presented by HGTV—while perusing the advice and wisdom that the designers and homeowners featured in this book have so graciously shared. Enjoy!

1 ROOM 3 WAYS

designers'challenge changesonthesurface

The 10 rooms featured in this section show how paint, fabric, flooring, and other easy-to-achieve surface changes can make a powerful design statement. You'll see how new furniture arrangements can increase the functionality of a room, enhance traffic flow, create decorative focal points, highlight the architectural assets of your home, and take better advantage of existing views.

1 ROOM
3 WAYS

designers'challenge comfort for a **crowd**

BEFORE THE MAKEOVER

Jerome and Karen Byrd challenged designers to restyle their large, boring living room into a welcoming gathering space that would oblige both entertaining and relaxing—on a budget of $20,000.

DESIGNERS JACKIE FILTZER BAYER & JESSICA GLYNN, MERCHANDISING EAST

FOCUS ON THE PIANO. Jerome and Karen Byrd's living room was roomy and window-filled, but it lacked the warmth the couple desired. In Jackie and Jessica's plan, fabric and accessories soften the hard lines of the room. "Our plan accommodates the Byrds' request to make their grand piano a focal point of the room, as well as their desire to provide seating for eight or more," Jackie says.

WARM EARTH TONES. "The wooded views framed by the living room windows dictate the color palette," Jessica explains. The palette includes sage greens, dusty corals, and sands. A new cream-color carpet ties the color scheme together while brightening the room. "Neutral fabrics on the primary furnishings create a very open and airy feel, while the accent pieces pop color into the room," Jessica says.

VISIBLE TEXTURE. To add texture and color to the one wall that isn't cedar, the designers suggest covering it with a faux-suede sage-green paint treatment. A vanilla glaze lightens the brick on the grand fireplace chimney without affecting its architectural integrity.

MAXIMUM LIGHT. Because privacy isn't an issue on the wooded lot, window treatments frame the window but do not inhibit the view. Track lights enhance the daylight that spills through the tall windows.

FLEXIBLE SEATING. "The furnishings can be easily rearranged to suit most occasions," Jackie says. The clean lines of the furnishings complement the architecture of the room and match the style preferences of the homeowners.

THE BYRD RESIDENCE

"To ensure we understand the needs and desires of our clients, we often ask them to pull pages from magazines that illustrate their tastes."

JESSICA GLYNN

2

DESIGNER LINDSAY FLOWER NCIDQ, ANN LINDSAY INTERIORS, INC.

A PLACE TO GATHER. Lindsay envisions a music appreciation area near the windows and another gathering area around the fireplace, with plenty of comfortable seating for all. "I want to create a warm and comfortable space for the Byrds to gather with family and friends," Lindsay says.

FOCAL-POINT VIEW. "My plan takes advantage of the room's key elements: the bank of windows that provides a view of lush green lawn and the tranquil woods beyond, as well as the cathedral ceiling and the enormous fireplace surround," Lindsay explains. Fabrics and colors accentuate the view.

FORMAL FURNITURE. Furnishings include a pale beige sofa and matching love seat—both in a traditional style—as well as a carved wooden French-style chair covered in a floral-motif fabric. Throw pillows in a deep green on the sofa and loveseat add color and a touch of whimsy. Upholstered furnishings are complemented by a carved wooden coffee table, a small chest of drawers, and a curved sofa table.

EYE-CATCHING FIREPLACE. Chairs upholstered in a deep red fabric grace the seating area in front of the fireplace. To help create a focal point above the fireplace, Lindsay recommends a circa-1930s French poster to add style, grace, and color to the wide brick chimney.

ACCENT LIGHTING. Lamps on either side of the sofa add intimacy during the evening hours. Uplights illuminate the floor plants that visually soften the corners of the room.

"My passion is to blend a fabulous aesthetic, such as fabric, with practicality."   LINDSAY FLOWER

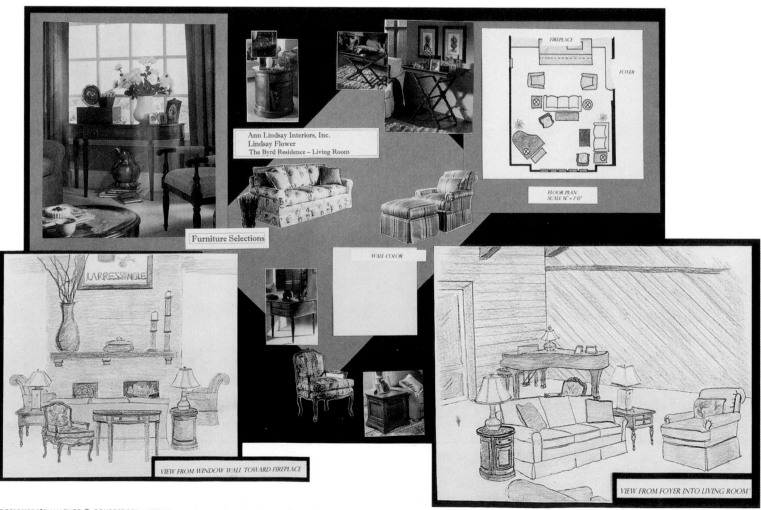

Ann Lindsay Interiors, Inc.
Lindsay Flower
The Byrd Residence – Living Room

FIREPLACE

FOYER

FLOOR PLAN
SCALE ¼" = 1'0"

Furniture Selections

WALL COLOR

VIEW FROM WINDOW WALL TOWARD FIREPLACE

VIEW FROM FOYER INTO LIVING ROOM

3 DESIGNER VICTOR LIBERATORE ASID, VICTOR LIBERATORE INTERIOR DESIGN

BEAUTIFUL LIGHTING. Victor's redesign includes an expansive lighting system that will illuminate the room, which is filled with vibrant fabrics. A cable system, which runs parallel to the ceiling beams, attaches to dimmers that allow control over the amount of light in the room. "The cable fixtures themselves are custom-made in a style to complement the decor of the room," Victor explains.

MULTIPLE FOCAL POINTS. Focal points include a new custom mantel that is in scale with the fireplace and the grand piano. "As you enter into the space, your eye will naturally be drawn to the piano and adjacent views," Victor says. The windows opposite the fireplace feature a cornice upholstered in a floral-motif fabric. Cascades of a sheer fabric drape the top third of the windowpanes to add a hint of softness. A four-panel screen is positioned along a cedar wall to add composition to the space. An indoor water fountain connects the interior to the lush view seen through the wall of windows.

CROWD CONTROL. Furnishings accommodate up to 11 people. A soft green chenille-covered sofa sits adjacent to two rattan side chairs and a skirted table that is covered in a matching fabric. Throw pillows in soft green, pale yellow, and creamy white prints encourage relaxation. A coffee table with a leaded-glass top anchors the arrangement. A star-shape ottoman covered in the same fabric as the sofa provides seating near the piano.

"Lighting is one of the most important aspects of any design; without proper lighting, the design falls flat." VICTOR LIBERATORE

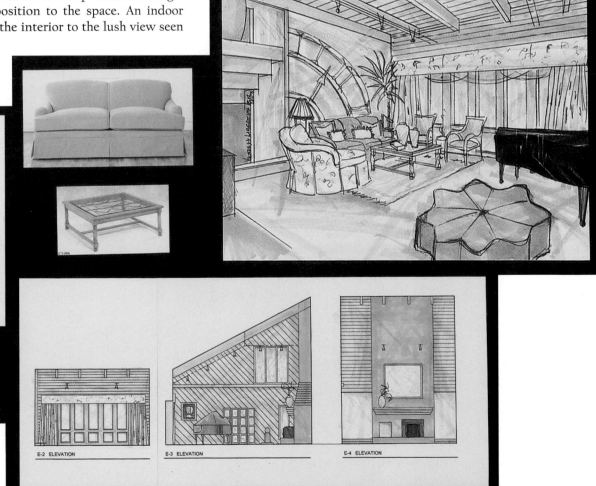

"Jackie and Jessica's plan captures the comfort and elegance we were looking for," homeowner Karen Byrd says. "The colors work perfectly with the cedar walls."

WHAT MAKES THIS PLAN WORK? A flexible furniture arrangement accommodates both small and large gatherings. A combination of occasional tables *below left* offers convenient landings for drinks and hors d'oeuvres. New wall sconces *right* enhance natural light.

Cream-color carpet lightens the overall look of the room and complements the fabrics on the floral side chairs *opposite*. The sage-green faux-suede textured wall also blends with the fabric colors and offsets the lush forest greens in the view. Cornices and drapery panels frame the enticing view and balance the fireplace on the flanking wall *below right*. "The fireplace is one of the things that changed the most," Jackie says. Although the Byrds decided against the original plan for glazing the bricks, the designers increased the heft of the mantelpiece to offset the wide surround.

HOW CAN YOU GET THE LOOK? To instill a similar look in your living room, choose a rich floral-print fabric, such as the one used on the Byrds' chairs, and let it define all the other colors in your room. "If necessary have paint custom-blended to match your fabric selections and existing woodwork," Jessica says. "It's much easier than finding a fabric to match the paint."

DID THE DESIGNERS MEET THE BUDGET? Jessica says they used every bit of the allotted budget, but not a penny more. "We wanted to give the Byrds all the amenities they desired without going over budget," Jackie says. "That is something we take pride in doing for all our clients. We shop various manufacturer lines so that we are able to get the most value out of each dollar spent." **ACTUAL COST** $20,000

"The room is great for unwinding as well as entertaining. The dual purposes make the space even more valuable to us," Karen Byrd says.

INVESTING IN FURNITURE

The fabric of an upholstered piece is the most visible sign of quality and also the part most likely to show wear or age. Fabric cost does not necessarily reflect quality, Jessica cautions. Heavy fabrics, such as leather, canvas, tapestry, and woven wool (shown on the sofa *right*), are generally more durable than lightweight fabrics, such as taffeta, chintz, and linen. Save lighter-weight fabrics for throw pillows and side chairs *opposite* or padded benches that are used less frequently.

Unless the frame is solid and well-made, the piece—whether a sofa or a chair—won't stand the test of time. Kiln-dried hardwoods, such as birch, maple, and ash, are signs of a quality frame. Soft, lightweight woods, such as pine, are not as sturdy. Wood joints should be mortise-and-tenon (where one slot-shape piece of wood slides into another) or dovetail (where wood fingers lock together like gears) and secured with glue. These joints are much stronger than butted and screwed joints. Avoid furniture that shows buckling between parts such as the cushions and frame, the fitted pillow and arm, or the wooden and upholstered parts. Squeeze padded areas—you shouldn't be able to feel the frame.

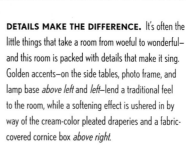

DETAILS MAKE THE DIFFERENCE. It's often the little things that take a room from woeful to wonderful—and this room is packed with details that make it sing. Golden accents—on the side tables, photo frame, and lamp base *above left* and *left*—lend a traditional feel to the room, while a softening effect is ushered in by way of the cream-color pleated draperies and a fabric-covered cornice box *above right*.

1 ROOM
3 WAYS

designers'challenge

room with a view

On a budget of $32,000, Brian and Suzie Campbell asked three designers to turn their impersonal living room into an attractive, functional gathering space.

BEFORE THE MAKEOVER

DESIGNER CONSTANCE RAMOS ALLIED ASID, RAMOS DESIGN CONSULTANTS

THREE-PART HARMONY. "The intriguing part of this project is that the room is beautifully directed toward the ocean," Constance says. To make the room more functional, she proposes dividing it into three parts. The first is a casual space where the family can watch television together. The second is a transitional area that houses a convenient beverage and serving center. The third is a seating area arranged to take full advantage of the panoramic view. All the walls throughout the three areas are painted in one of two shades of yellow.

FAMILY GATHERING. A colorful area rug with geometric motifs marks the perimeter of the casual space. A sunny yellow leather sectional sofa with a chaise lounge, an oversize chair covered in earthy red chenille, and two large leather ottomans are the primary furnishings. Two existing contemporary chairs are refurbished with chocolate-color leather to offer additional seating. A pale birch mantel and a limestone veneer update the variegated marble surround of the fireplace.

SNACK SERVICE. A new L-shape birch bar with a glass top defines the transitional area. Open shelves and lighted displays are built into the bar. Custom-made, handblown glass pendant light fixtures provide task and mood lighting.

SEATING FOR THE VIEW. A pair of contemporary sofas and a custom-made chair-for-two define the formal seating area. A sofa table provides display space for candles and greenery. Sheer sunscreen shades soften the harsh late-afternoon sun without inhibiting the view.

"I am passionate about using technological freedom to evoke any kind of response we wish with our built environment."

CONSTANCE RAMOS

2

DESIGNER JAMES SWAN, JAMES SWAN AND COMPANY, INC.

WOW, GREAT ROOM. "Brian and Suzie Campbell's living room is a big, rambling space that doesn't have a real sense of unity," James says. "When you walk into the space now, you say, 'Wow, great view.' What I'd like to see happen is that you say, 'Wow, great room. Wow, great view.'"

ENVELOPING AMBIENCE. James's vision for the room is to wrap the walls and the ceiling beams in a cozy caramel color that is a few shades darker than the existing carpet. The fireplace receives a complete makeover and is reduced from a width of 36 inches to about 18 inches. A contemporary wire sculpture adorns the wall above a new natural-stone surround. The room is divided into three areas: TV viewing, display, and conversation near the view.

TV SCENE. An L-shape sectional sofa upholstered in an bark-color cotton twill provides a clear view of the big-screen TV and the fireplace. An overstuffed reading chair in a complementary fabric fills a corner by the fireplace and swivels to offer a view of the TV.

AMPLE DISPLAY SPACE. New built-in bookcases on the opposite side of the fireplace connect to a matching built-in bar that seats two. Opposite the bar, a wide glass display—included at the request of the Campbells—provides space to showcase greenery and statuary.

OBSERVATION LOUNGE. James refers to the remaining section of the room as the "observation area," where two chaise lounges are oriented toward the ocean. Round-top hand-carved walnut occasional tables in a variety of sizes are sprinkled throughout the seating areas to hold reading lamps and accessories. Several potted palm trees bring a sense of the outdoors inside.

"My design philosophy is summed up in three words: appropriate, appropriate, appropriate. If it's appropriate for our client's lifestyle, appropriate for the architecture, and appropriate for the natural setting, then it works."

JAMES SWAN

3

DESIGNER CHARLIE PLATERO JR. ALLIED ASID, CHARLIE PLATERO JR. INTERIOR DESIGN

CLEAN LINES. "My vision for the Campbells' living room is a very clean, straightforward, and sophisticated design," Charlie says. Carefully staged furniture extends the current media area closer to the existing bar. A brown leather sectional sofa with a chaise on one end and a pair of armless oversize chairs in a cheerful geometric print fabric are angled in the new arrangement so guests can enjoy both the fireplace and the television. A trio of square zebrawood coffee tables is arranged corner-to-corner in the center of the seating area to create a diamond pattern. Wide crown molding gives the existing media center more prominence in the room.

EXTREME MAKEOVER. The fireplace chimney is resurfaced with drywall that's painted in a faux-suede of creams and rusty reds. The same red is used on the trimwork throughout the living room. A rustic brown granite covers the existing hearth.

"Creativity is what sets a great design apart from a good one." CHARLIE PLATERO JR.

SURFACE CHANGE. Charlie maintains the layout of the existing bar but adds two small ottomans that can be used as stools. A new granite top matches the fireplace hearth.

TEXTURAL INTEGRITY. The end of the room is furnished with two extrawide mocha-color chenille chairs with low backs and a large round wooden coffee table. Two large ottomans covered in a contrasting contemporary-print fabric can be used for additional seating. Charlie suggests solar shades accented by copper mesh panels that resemble draperies.

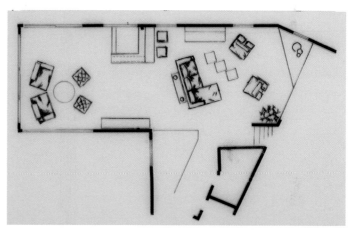

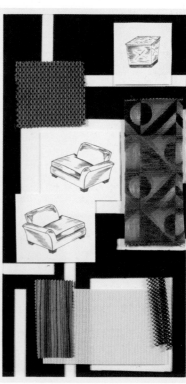

"Constance's plan reflected exactly what Suzie and I were trying to accomplish," homeowner Brian Campbell says. "Her creativity and communication skills made us confident of a successful outcome."

WHAT MAKES THIS PLAN WORK? Brian and Suzie's living room *left* and *below* is now a warm, colorful, and enticing space. Seating in the entertainment area alone provides room for eight. A new stone veneer on the fireplace transforms the dated original into a timeless focal point. Open shelves on the outside of the new bar provide more storage and display space. Furnishings throughout the room are comfortable enough for relaxing and durable enough for kids and pets.

HOW CAN YOU GET THE LOOK? "What makes the Campbells' living room so special is that it reflects the owners' personalities while enhancing the architecture of the home," Constance explains. Quality craftsmanship is apparent in everything from the custom-made chandelier to the placement of the stone tiles. To create a very personal look in your own home, Constance suggests you throw caution to the wind and choose colors and finishes that your family members love instead of what you think the neighbors might like.

DID THE DESIGNER MEET THE BUDGET? The Campbells increased their budget to add a second chandelier above the stairwell (not shown) and to upgrade the fireplace facade. **ACTUAL COST** $34,000

BEFORE THE MAKEOVER

"Brian and Suzie love color and texture, so we were able to fill their living room with cheerful hues and tactile furnishings that highlight both the contemporary architecture and the family's personalities," designer Constance Ramos says.

DESIGN HARMONY

Your design plan should enhance, not overtake, the interior architecture of your home. The sleek furnishings and natural surfaces in the Campbells' 1982 home are in harmony with the contemporary oceanside structure. Imagine the discord that would have been created if the designer opted to include carved Georgian columns or spindly Victorian fretwork in this living room. Follow the same theory of enhancement when choosing new surfaces and moldings and, when possible, spread these enhancements throughout the interior of your home to create continuity in your design.

BEFORE THE MAKEOVER

BEFORE THE MAKEOVER

WARM AND CONTEMPORARY. That's not an oxymoron when describing the Campbells' new living space *this photo, opposite left,* and *opposite right.* Sunny yellows warm the walls throughout the room, and cheerful reds accent the furnishings and accessories. Textures abound throughout the space: the limestone fireplace veneer, the smooth birch cabinets, the patterned areas rugs, and the tufted-leather furnishings.

"The living room is usable now," Brian Campbell says. "Both seating arrangements are comfortable, inviting, and durable enough for us to use every day."

WINDOW TO THE WORLD. The fabric colors are muted, and the accessories are minimal in the viewing area *this photo* to keep the focus on the view. Birch bar cabinets *opposite* complement the existing wood steps and built-ins. The light fixture above the bar was custom-made to complement the new decor and the existing fixture in the raised dining area beyond.

1 ROOM 3 WAYS

smallspaces, smartstyle

Navin and Becky Narang invited three designers to add Tuscan flair to an unused living room and the adjacent entryway with a budget of $25,000.

BEFORE THE MAKEOVER

DESIGNER SUE GORMAN, SUE GORMAN INTERIOR DESIGNS

ALFRESCO THEME. Sue's plan creates a visual gateway to the outdoors as well as a dramatic first impression in Navin and Becky Narang's two-year-old home. A water element in each niche in the entry rotunda offers soothing sound and visual interest the moment the Narangs and guests step in the door. Coffee-color faux-suede textured walls in the rotunda complement the fabrics in the living room. Floor-to-ceiling curtains in a fabric that is the same color as the walls add softness around the windows and highlight the view.

WALNUT FLOOR. A new custom black walnut floor replaces the living room carpet and visually brings the height of the room down, making the space feel cozier.

FOCAL-POINT FIREPLACE. The slate surround of the fireplace is extended to the floor, and the facade is painted a deep brown.

FLEXIBLE SEATING. A classically styled sofa and two easy-to-move chairs surround the fireplace and offer seating for four. The sofa fabric combines the colors used in this room and throughout the Narang home. Four leather-covered cubes bunch together to serve as a coffee table but can also be separated to provide additional seating. Various wooden occasional tables provide storage and display space; padded benches stored beneath the tables pull out for even more seating.

NIGHT LIGHT. Table and floor lamps provide task lighting and ambience. A circular central light fixture complements the round walls in the entry rotunda.

"I use color and continuity to bring a project from what the clients have to what the clients want." SUE GORMAN

2

DESIGNER BETH WHITLINGER ASID, IIDA, CID, BETH WHITLINGER INTERIOR DESIGN

UPSCALE TROPICS. "In keeping with the other spaces in the Narang home, the design needs to be comfortable and yet formal," Beth says. Her plan combines an upscale tropical theme with a rustic Italian style already present throughout the remainder of the home.

ITALIAN GARDEN. The living room seating arrangement is anchored by an olive-green-color love seat with tropical-print throw pillows and four side chairs covered in merlot-tone fabrics. The couple's piano is repositioned so that the keys are visible from the rotunda—providing the most interesting view of the instrument. Several large tropical plants fill the tranquil space with life.

WELCOME TEXTURE. A wooden side table with a leather top and hand-rubbed iron side tables bring texture into the room. Another round table, centered in the rotunda, offers a spot to display fresh flowers or a prized work of art. The existing carpet remains in the room: "Its basket-weave pattern and golden tones complement the new design and make the room warm and inviting," Beth explains.

COLOR-WASHED WALLS AND CEILINGS. Walls color-washed in golden and bronze hues visually lower the high ceiling in the living room and create a cocoonlike feel. The coffered ceiling in the rotunda is hand-painted to resemble the morning sky.

OLD-WORLD FIREPLACE. The faux-finished mantel and wooden surround are painted to match the frames of the side chairs. Mosaic tiles, bronzed iridescent glass, and a slate hearth matching the rotunda floor complete the focal-point fireplace.

ACCENT LIGHTING. Recessed lights accentuate the hearth, piano, and sitting area. Wrought-iron chandeliers illuminate the piano and the rotunda. Table and floor lamps with tropical flair complete the ethereal lighting scheme.

ARCHITECTURAL HIGHLIGHTS. Painted casings—instead of window treatments—maximize the view of the newly landscaped yard. Matching crown molding outlines the ceiling, while base molding brings emphasis to the floor.

"My strength as a designer is in color selection. I'm able to work a lot of colors into an environment and make it gel."

BETH WHITLINGER

DESIGNER SHAWN HAYES ASID, HAYES INTERIOR DESIGN

FORMALWEAR. "I want this space to reflect Navin and Becky, all dressed up," Shawn says. Her plan blends heavily textured fabrics and warm colors to create a sophisticated and welcoming space.

OUTDOOR CONNECTION. French doors replace the center windows on the main windowed wall. "I concentrated most of the furniture on one side of the room so that traffic could flow around the piano to the door," Shawn explains. Floor-to-ceiling draperies, hung just outside the windowpanes, accentuate the view without obstructing it.

EASY ARRANGEMENT. "I chose armless chairs and a small sofa to make the room feel more open and spacious," Shawn says. Bombay tables offer storage and display space. A buffet with a marble or granite top fills one corner and doubles as a serving bar. For the wall treatment, a faux finish mixes the existing warm yellow wall color with greens and creams, creating a textural look.

A TRIO OF ARTWORK. Three new Italian prints that emulate the look of old tapestries adorn the wall above the fireplace, drawing attention to the existing focal point. The round mirror that previously hung above the fireplace is now relocated behind the sofa to reflect the backyard view.

FINISHING TOUCHES. An Italian chandelier and table lamps bring ambient and task lighting into the room and accentuate the formal design theme. Beeswax candles, upscale iron planters, and hand-painted Italian pottery accessorize the room with classic flavor.

Narang Residence Formal Living Room

Narang Residence Formal Living Room

"I am most passionate about furniture. You can really make a space open up and smile when you use great fabrics on classic pieces."

SHAWN HAYES

2

"Beth's plan fit our personalities best: It has a tropical feel and yet it is formal enough to fit our vision," homeowner Navin Narang explains.

WHAT MAKES THIS PLAN WORK? Repositioning the piano to the left of the entryway opens up floor space in the living room *right*. Four cushioned side chairs can be arranged to focus on the piano, the fireplace, or the view. A small sofa placed perpendicular to the fireplace can seat up to three adults. The combination of furnishings offers the Narangs and their guests multiple seating options. A handmade iron table centered below a matching iron chandelier provides a focal-point display spot in the rotunda *opposite*. Existing slate tiles, laid in a circular pattern, complement the curved walls.

HOW CAN YOU GET THE LOOK? Texture draws people into a gathering room almost as much as the smell of baking cookies draws them to the kitchen, Beth says. To dress up your living spaces, apply a finish to the walls that mimics suede or leather, then add fabrics that range from soft and nubby to silky and smooth.

DID THE DESIGNER MEET THE BUDGET? Beth saved the Narangs money by updating the windows with moldings instead of more costly custom fabric window treatments. Keeping the existing carpet in the living room enabled the designer to spend more on hand-painted finishes and still keep the budget in check.

ACTUAL COST $25,000

BEFORE THE MAKEOVER

"We jumped the gun and bought a baby grand piano before we bought furniture. We needed a professional to come up with a way to furnish the living room around it," Navin Narang says.

TOUCHABLE TEXTURE

A room filled with texture as shown *left* and *opposite* subtly delights the senses of sight and touch. For touchable impact forget matching and mix in as many different textures as possible. Pair hard and soft, ribbed and smooth, fuzzy and silky, coarse and fine. Experiment with various textiles, from crisp chintzes to feathery velvets, then toss in a few nubby weaves as wake-up calls for your senses.

As you mix, keep in mind that soft silks, cuddly cashmeres, and sheer lace generally cast a romantic spell, while rugged textures, such as leather, wool, and canvas, create a more masculine mood. Encircle a smooth wooden or glass tabletop with bamboo, wicker, or hand-forged iron as shown on the table *left*. Toss a chenille throw onto a nubby wool sofa. Position a rough-hewn floor lamp next to a silk-covered side chair.

COLOR CONNECTIONS. Golden color-washed walls *above* bring earthy texture to the living room walls. Deep cherry moldings around the windows draw attention to the view and complement the finish on the existing baby grand piano and new side tables. Similar cherry moldings adorn the perimeter of the floor and the ceiling. Exotic green plants *above* and earthy handmade pottery pieces *opposite* connect the indoor space to the view beyond.

BEFORE THE MAKEOVER

"We had to redo the faux-suede finish on the walls a couple times to achieve the finish we wanted, but the extra effort was worth the final result," designer Beth Whitlinger says.

MANTEL MAKEOVER. Mosaic tiles in a variety of patterns draw attention to the new fireplace surround *opposite* and complement the slate floor in the adjacent rotunda. The heavily textured painted mantel finish mimics the metallic finish on the cushioned chairs *right* and complements the hand-forged iron tables. A pair of Italian prints hangs above the mantel to bring eye-pleasing balance to the focal point, which was previously overpowered by an oversize mirror *below*. Accessories include a trio of candle pedestals and an old iron dinner bell, which sits on top of the mantel.

BEFORE THE MAKEOVER

BEFORE THE MAKEOVER

1 ROOM
3 WAYS

fine french living

Brian and Kelly Muir asked designers to turn their cavernous living room into a sophisticated French retreat on a budget of $30,000.

BEFORE THE MAKEOVER

DESIGNERS SANDY CRAIG & CHRISTY HOPPLE, RYAN TAYLORS INTERIOR DESIGN

PERIOD PERFECTION. "Brian and Kelly Muir's living room has a nice foundation we can build on: a beautiful wood floor and a cozy fireplace," Christy says. The design team's inspiration for the remainder of the room comes from the 1940s, the decade during which the Muirs' home was built, linking the room to the architecture of the home. "By bringing the look of the exterior architecture inside, we are able to bring a period feel into the space," Sandy explains.

ACCENT RUG. A beautiful French wool rug with a scroll motif defines the new layout, which is anchored in one corner by a baby grand piano. Opposite the piano, a built-in bookcase becomes a custom-made beverage station. An angled chaise lounge and the existing brown leather club chair and ottoman fill the remaining corners of the room and provide comfortable seating for the Muirs and their guests. A round, thickly padded ottoman provides additional seating by the piano. A tufted, silk-upholstered screen adds drama to the corner behind the club chair.

ELABORATE DETAILS. A dramatically coffered ceiling features low-voltage lighting around the perimeter and recessed spotlights that accentuate the focal points of the room. A creamy silk tone-on-tone wall covering brings color and texture to the living room walls. The ceiling is painted in a color that matches the wall covering. The existing brick fireplace is refaced with sparkling black granite. New half-glass slatted doors enclose the entrance to the room and complement the existing slatted double doors that connect the space to the dining room. Formal drapery panels made from silk in a burnt-salmon color draw attention to the floor-to-ceiling windows.

"There are three aspects of design people need to address: color, texture, and balance. Balance comes from accessorizing."

SANDY CRAIG

"You need accent pieces to personalize and bring a room together. I think that's what most people struggle with when they design a room themselves."

CHRISTY HOPPLE

2

DESIGNER CASSANDRA KREPS ASSOCIATE IIDA, CASSANDRA KREPS INTERIOR DESIGN AND DESIGN SPECIALITY, LLC

HISTORICAL ACCURACY. Cassandra's plan features a rustic feel with historically accurate details. "My design embodies the ambience of a 1930s French club," Cassandra explains.

A BLEND OF OLD AND NEW. A small love seat and a French slipper chair complement the two club chairs the Muirs already have. Glass shelves and interior lighting enhance the existing built-in bookcase. A new French console, topped in black marble, provides storage for glasses and beverages.

STRIKING FIREPLACE. The same marble that enhances the console covers the fireplace surround and mantel. The color and texture of the marble strike a pleasing balance against the shiny black finish of the new baby grand piano. Cassandra also suggests refinishing and extending the wooden fireplace facade to the ceiling to create a dramatic focal point for artwork. A matching dark finish is proposed for the remainder of the existing woodwork.

INSTANT AGE. Glazed walls have texture and depth that resemble aged plaster. A period reproduction wallpaper border crowns the room. Silk drapery panels with a narrow stripe motif frame the windows.

"I love working with period style. I love researching and finding out about the history of the furnishings of the time." CASSANDRA KREPS

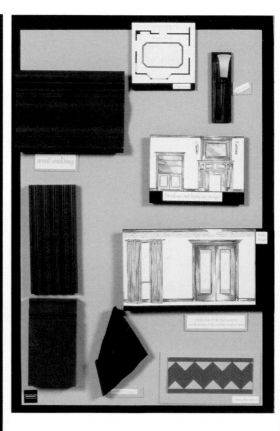

DESIGNER MIGUEL ANGEL ZAVALA, FOUND GALLERY

FLEXIBLE LAYOUT. "Brian and Kelly Muir have a design concept that doesn't really flow with the remainder of the house," Miguel says. "I'm looking forward to changing their minds." His contemporary plan revolves around a flexible seating layout that's designed to accommodate entertaining.

SEATING FOR SEVERAL. Upholstered in two complementary fabrics, a custom-designed sectional sofa can be reconfigured in a variety of ways to seat multiple guests. Throw pillows made from three additional fabrics add interest to the versatile piece. A stool made of walnut and twin leather ottomans offer additional seating.

EXTENDED FLOOR SPACE. Instead of allowing room for a baby grand piano as the couple requested, Miguel suggests using an ornate upright piano to conserve floor space and enhance an open and airy feel. Rail-mounted doors cover the main entrance to the room.

NEUTRAL COLOR SCHEME. Limestone pavers cover the existing bricks on the fireplace surround and accentuate the new taupe color scheme of the room. The wooden fireplace facade and woodwork throughout the space is painted in a darker shade of taupe. Wallpaper custom-made by Miguel brings texture and color to the walls.

NATURAL TEXTURE. A custom area rug is made of mountain grass. Wooden matchstick window blinds combine with dark brown draperies to create earth-tone window coverings. Three candlelit wall sconces provide dramatic accent lighting.

"What I love about being a designer is making a space flow, making a space work, and seeing the client's joy when the space is complete."

MIGUEL ZAVALA

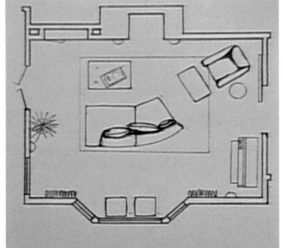

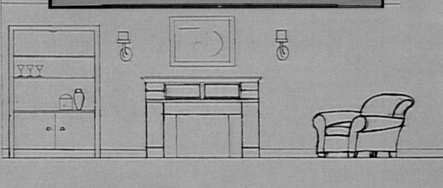

"Christy and Sandy's plan gave us everything we asked for, plus a few welcome surprises," homeowner Kelly Muir says. White woodwork offsets the richly colored silk wallpaper and the existing hardwood floors.

WHAT MAKES THIS PLAN WORK? As suggested in the designers' original plan, a scroll-motif rug anchors the furniture arrangement, which includes a classic French chaise lounge *opposite* and the Muirs' existing leather club chair. A similar scroll design adorns the iron fireplace screen and the iron accents on the new glass doors, bringing a sense of continuity to the space. "The glass doors are different than the ones we originally suggested, but they better complement the room's ornate design," Sandy explains. A large skirted ottoman *right* tucks under the piano and can be pulled out to use as an extra seat or table.

HOW CAN YOU GET THE LOOK? "To make a period design look and feel authentic to the space, you need to do some homework," Sandy says. Go to the library and look through books on historical architecture and design. Tie these historical elements to the architecture of your home, highlighting existing features such as archways or bump-outs. Choose an accent color or a signature fabric, such as the rich silk used in the Muirs' living room, to spread color and drama throughout the space.

DID THE DESIGNERS MEET THE BUDGET? Christy and Sandy priced each item in their plan to make sure it fit within the allotted budget before making their final presentation to Kelly and Brian. Although the Muirs did select a few alternate fabrics and finishes, the couple chose comparably priced replacements, keeping the project on budget.

ACTUAL COST $30,000

"The Muirs' painting of a 1940s French nightclub was the inspiration for the design of this room and gave us a very clear picture of what the owners wanted," designer Sandy Craig says.

"When I first saw the vibrant colors of the rug, I was a little frightened by it," homeowner Brian Muir says. "Once the rest of the fabrics and furnishings were installed, I could see how beautifully it all works together."

MAKE IT PERSONAL

The Muirs' cabaret-style living room speaks volumes about the homeowners' tastes and passions for the colors and decoration of times past. Do you have an interest in interiors that look decades or even centuries old? If you do but aren't sure how to start personalizing your living spaces, look to decorating books, magazines, and television shows to provide ideas on accessories and personal style. Take your favorite pictures on shopping trips to show designers or sales associates the looks you like best. Enhance purchased pieces with accents that tell a personal story. The story can be literal—perhaps told by photographs that show you and your family over the years—or anecdotal—a tale brought to life through treasured collectibles that jog wonderful memories and become conversation pieces as you recount their origins to guests. Whether written in words or spotlighted in design, the best stories have a point. Edit out extraneous objects that clutter your intended message.

BEFORE THE MAKEOVER

BEFORE THE MAKEOVER

VISUAL CONNECTIONS. Design details that repeat create a cohesive look. In the Muirs' new living room *above left*, scroll patterns are duplicated in the area rug, in the iron inserts in the glass door *opposite above left*, and in the iron fireplace screen *opposite above right*. Vases and plant stands *opposite below left* feature equally ornate carvings. Throw pillow fabrics *opposite below right* connect all the upholstered pieces, window coverings, and accessories by repeating color combinations.

1 ROOM
3 WAYS

designers'challenge everyday work & play

BEFORE THE MAKEOVER

Jeff Gonzer and Nora Freedman challenged designers to completely rework their living room and adjacent office with a budget of $25,000.

DESIGNER LAUREN JACOBSEN, JACOBSEN DESIGN

COUPLE COMFORT. "Jeff Gonzer and Nora Freedman's home is a great challenge because they have some really specific needs, especially in the office," Lauren says. To create ample work space for two, Lauren's layout includes a large laminated L-shape desk that wraps around one corner of the office. Open shelves and storage cubbies above the desk provide extra storage and display space. A second modular workstation stands in the opposite corner. A padded window seat provides a spot for contemplation and relaxation. A sisal rug with a floral-motif border adds comfort and durability underfoot.

PUPPY COMFORT. A dog bed enables the couple's dog to rest in the room while they work.

HERE AND THERE. Woven wooden shades control light in both the office and living room; the living room blinds are topped with a contemporary triangular-shape treatment that draws more attention to the wall of windows. The walls are painted a shade of butterscotch; the living room walls are painted a slightly darker shade than the office to make the gathering space feel cozier. Accent fabrics, pottery pieces, and artwork in both rooms feature earthy wheats, browns, greens, and taupes.

CONTEMPORARY COCOON. The living room receives a contemporary-style sofa and swiveling side chairs; an Asian area rug completes the conversation grouping. Fabrics in similar shades tie the spaces together. A mosaic travertine tile fireplace facade and a new wider hearth update the fireplace.

ASIAN ACCENTS. The television and audiovisual equipment fit inside an 18th-century Asian armoire. Large Asian vases and a mirror with a wide frame draw attention to the focal-point mantel. A variety of Asian-inspired occasional tables, lamps, and accessories completes the design.

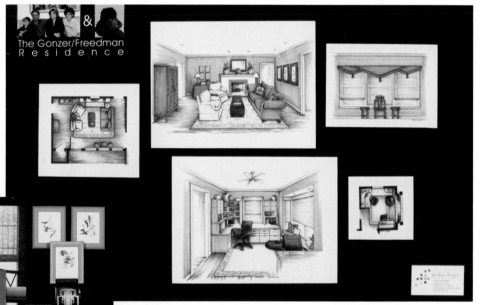

The Gonzer/Freedman Residence

"I love to come in and make somebody's life more comfortable, more relaxed, and more efficient."

LAUREN JACOBSEN

2

DESIGNER CHARLIE PLATERO JR. ALLIED ASID, CHARLIE PLATERO JR. INTERIOR DESIGN

CLEAN LINES. Charlie's sophisticated plan emphasizes clean, contemporary lines. In the living room a chaise lounge, a coffee table, two armless chairs, and an occasional table make up the primary seating area. Two padded ottomans, placed against the wall opposite the front door, can be pulled up to create more seating when needed.

SMALLER FIREPLACE. The fireplace facade width is shortened from 8 to 6 feet; this reduction in the size and scale of the facade better complements the seating area. A white wood mantel and a honed-stone surround and hearth make the fireplace a focal point. Sconces are installed on opposites sides of the hearth.

UNITED FRONT. In the office two custom workstations flank the window opposite the door. Ergonomically designed chairs provide hours of comfort—an important factor when working at home. Wall storage units keep supplies and reference materials handy. Another chaise lounge provides a spot for relaxing while reading or talking on the phone.

DEEP COLORS. Fabrics in shades of coffee, wine, gold, and black; white plantation shutters; jute rugs; and a hand-painted floor border unite the living room and office.

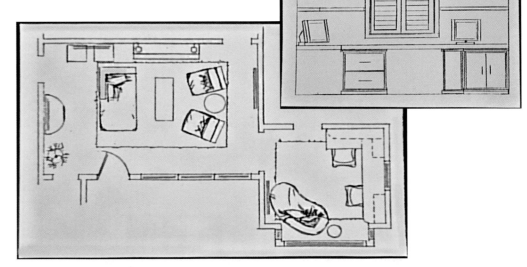

"My passion for design is to give all I can by thinking of creative, innovative ways to make a positive impact on the attitude of a room."

CHARLIE PLATERO JR.

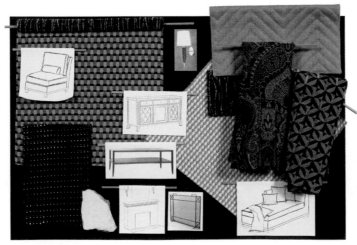

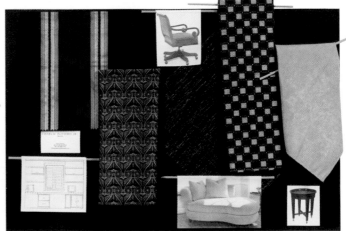

3

DESIGNERS KENNETH DEAN & SHAYNA BELL, DEAN INTERNATIONAL DESIGNS

ENGLISH LIBRARY. Kenneth and Shayna propose a classic formal living room and an office with the traditional look of an English library.

TRADITIONAL FIREPLACE FACADE. "When you walk in the front door, the focal point is the fireplace," Kenneth says. "We would redo it in a combination of wood and marble or with a light stone mantel in a size that better fits the seating area."

CUSTOM FURNITURE. The furniture in both rooms is custom-fabricated with a variety of options for fabric and finishes. Flanking sofas separated by a centered coffee table are proposed for the living room. A geometric-print area rug warms the floor and defines the seating area.

DUAL WORKSTATIONS. The office features a custom L-shape desk with two workstations. Roll-top appliance garages can be pulled down to conceal the computers. Seating options include a window seat and a more formal club chair.

WARM PALETTES. Color suggestions include a palette of deep berry reds and blacks or moss greens and taupes. Wooden shutters, finished in a warm honey tone, cover the windows in both rooms.

"A room is complete when the designer is long gone and the client walks into that room, sits down in that chair, and says 'this feels like home.'"

KENNETH DEAN

"It was amazing how three different design firms approached the decorating of these two rooms so differently," homeowner Jeff Gonzer says. "Lauren was the designer who picked up on our personal tastes, so we chose her."

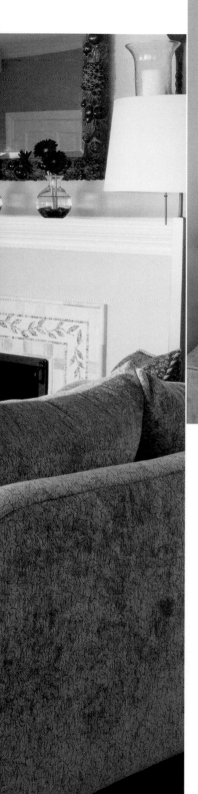

WHAT MAKES THIS PLAN WORK? In the living room *far left* a love seat and two overstuffed club chairs provide comfy seating for the couple and as many as four guests. New artwork and collectibles *left* pick up on the couple's appreciation for Far East design. In the office two separate work centers built in opposite corners of the room enable Jeff and Nora to work in the space at the same time without bumping elbows. Recessed lighting fixtures in both rooms supplement natural light and ease eye strain.

HOW CAN YOU GET THE LOOK? The couple's existing collections have a contemporary Asian flair. Their preferences guided the selection of accessories and artwork for these two rooms, Lauren explains. When redoing a room of your own, identify the furnishings and accessories in your personal collections that you like the best, and then look for common elements among these pieces. Are they of a similar color or shape? Are they intricately detailed or decidedly simple? Once you have determined what draws you to the items, shop for complementary pieces. To save costly mistakes, envision how these pieces will work in your newly designed space prior to buying.

DID THE DESIGNER MEET THE BUDGET? An increase of the budget enabled the couple to upgrade the office furniture to traditional white cabinetry, a decision both Nora and Jeff are happy with. New lamps, additional Asian collectibles, and other custom touches also increased the cost. **ACTUAL COST** $35,000

"Lauren is very creative and flexible, and the artistic and complete design she gave us was amazing," homeowner Nora Freedman says.

PLEASING FURNITURE ARRANGEMENTS

In room design proportion refers to how furnishings look in relation to each other and to the room itself. The most eye-pleasing arrangements appear compatible in scale. For example in the arrangement *above* the compact size of the coffee table complements the scale of the love seat.

● To apply the principles of proportion to your furnishings, start with your largest piece of furniture, and then add furnishings that complement its size. A table and lamp may be proportionate to one another, but placed next to the sofa, they may look too large or small.

● Check the visual weight of furnishings. Even if two chairs are the same height, a spindly and delicate one looks awkward next to an overstuffed and chunky one.

● Compose tabletop displays that span at least one-third of the table diameter. Reserve disproportionally small collectibles for glass display cases or shadowboxes.

BEFORE THE MAKEOVER

FORM MEETS FUNCTION. The new living room *opposite* and office *this photo* are stylish and comfortable, a perfect match for the ambience and decor throughout the remainder of the home. Butterscotch-color walls create a feeling of warmth and serenity and set off the pristine white woodwork. Artwork and accessory colors in both rooms harmonize the decor.

1 ROOM 3 WAYS

classic & kid-friendly

BEFORE THE MAKEOVER

Jen and Adam Alonso asked designers to transform their sunroom and adjacent living room into inviting spaces that suit both formal and kid-friendly gatherings—within a budget of $40,000.

DESIGNERS SUZAN DECKER ROSS ALLIED ASID, & JANET MARIE THOMAS ASID, DECKER ROSS INTERIORS

FAMILY FUNCTION. "The sunroom should be a light and airy space for Jen and the entire family to enjoy. The adjacent living room requires equally kid-friendly furnishings and accommodations but with a more traditional look to satisfy Adam's desire for formality," Janet Marie says.

LIBRARY LOOK. To achieve these goals the design team proposes casual and comfortable rattan furnishings for the sunroom and a more formal library look for the living room. Accessories and detailing complement the architecture of the 1927 Dutch Colonial-style home.

MAXIMUM VIEW. The Alonsos' sunroom offers a stunning view of a wooded lawn and garden, so Suzan and Janet Marie propose minimal window treatments to maximize the expanses of glass in the room.

PERIOD FLOORING. Matte-finish floor tiles replace the existing ultrashiny tiles in the sunroom. The same tiles are used for the fireplace surround in the living room. Sisal rugs warm the tiles and define the furniture grouping in the sunroom. Existing oak floors in the living room are enhanced with a large Oriental rug.

UNIFYING PALETTE. A palette of pale yellows, soft greens, and deep reds invigorates both rooms, creating the cozy look Jen desires while uniting both rooms.

BUILT-IN STORAGE. The existing painted cabinetry in the family room is sanded and refinished with an earthy brown stain. A new librarylike storage surround frames a leather and paisley-print sofa.

"The benefit of working as a team is that more ideas come to fruition and eventually evolve into perfect solutions." SUZAN DECKER ROSS

DESIGNER RICHARD E. CARLE ASID, CHATEAU DESIGNS, INC.

2

FUNCTIONAL DIVIDE. Richard proposes a casual sunporch where the family can gather and a formal living room Jen and Adam can use for entertaining guests.

ART WALL. The proposed design details play up the existing architectural charm of the Dutch Colonial home. Such details include an old-fashioned art shelf along one wall. Dentil molding and painted paneling adorn the wall below the narrow shelf.

"My greatest strength as a designer is creating functional, comfortable spaces that people feel instantly at home in." RICHARD CARLE

NATURAL COLORS. Neutral-tone fabrics that resemble linen are durable enough to stand up to family use. Soft shades of terra-cotta, brown, and sage green accent both spaces.

QUALITY TIME. In the sunroom a game table that can be used for checkers, chess, and backgammon encourages family activities. A classically styled curved-back sofa and two wing-back chairs are positioned in the center of the living area, creating a formal conversational grouping.

SHADED WINDOWS. Reed-style Roman shades topped with fabric valances cover the windows and help control the heat of the sun in the enclosed porch. Cream-color travertine tiles replace the existing shiny ceramic tiles. In the living room the louvered wooden shades that currently flank the fireplace extend to the ceiling line, making the windows appear larger and drawing more attention to the entire fireplace wall.

3

DESIGNERS SUSAN TAYLOR ASID & CONNIE RHODES, TAYLOR DESIGNS UNLIMITED, INC.

OLD SOUTHERN STYLE. Susan and Connie visualize an old Southern-style sunroom filled with botanical-print fabrics and garden accents and a casually elegant living room with a focus on the family.

VISUAL SEPARATION. The front door of the Alonsos' home opens directly into the sunroom, so the designers propose adding a wrought-iron room divider to differentiate the entry from the remainder of the room.

FURNITURE RESTORATION. The wicker furnishings already in the sunroom are restored to complement a new hall tree added to the front entrance of the room. Additional pieces, including a wooden and wrought-iron coffee table and a sofa table, accentuate the restored furniture.

FLORAL VALANCES AND TROPICAL ACCENTS. The existing heavy formal draperies that do not fit the casual look of a sunroom are replaced with simple floral swag valances. Garden-theme accessories include birdcages and tropical accents.

RUSTIC FLOORING. Terra-cotta tiles cover the sunroom floor and update the fireplace hearth surround in the adjacent living room. Area rugs with matching motifs—round in the sunroom and rectangular in the living room—further unite the spaces, as do complementary wrought-iron light fixtures.

WINDOW SEAT. A centered seating arrangement in the living room accommodates entertaining and after-dinner conversation. A window seat disguises firewood storage.

MATCHING TABLES. A dark wooden cocktail table and a console that matches the couple's existing secretary are added to create a cohesive look in the living room. Additional shelves placed on top of the existing built-in bookcases draw attention to the focal point.

"Being as detail-oriented as we are ensures that everything is completed to the homeowners' satisfaction the first time." SUSAN TAYLOR

Alonso Sunroom

Alonso Living Room

Sunroom

Living Room

"Our goal is to give a garden look to the sunroom and a library look to the living room, and have them both work well together," designer Janet Marie Thomas says.

WHAT MAKES THIS PLAN WORK? The Alonsos chose the plan by Suzan Decker Ross and Janet Marie Thomas because of the durability of the chosen fabrics and furnishings as well as the library look proposed for the living room, shown on *pages 62–63.* "The plan accommodates Adam's request for formality and my request for coziness, creating the perfect solution for us," Jen explains. The new rooms are an inviting mix of the casual Florida lifestyle and the formal elegance often found in traditionally decorated homes. "The design works because it complements the existing architecture and the lifestyle of the owners," Suzan explains.

HOW CAN YOU GET THE LOOK? When redecorating your own home, Suzan recommends you enhance the existing architectural features, and then choose furnishings and accessories that complement the look while making your life easier. In the Alonsos' case, that means choosing cottage-style furnishings covered in fabrics that can withstand a spill or two. Rounded tables in the sunroom *left* are void of sharp corners, and the ottoman in the living room can serve as a footstool, a game table, or as a seat for kids.

DID THE DESIGNERS MEET THE BUDGET? Suzan and Janet Marie met the budget and the expectations of the Alonsos by modifying their initial design so that they could give the Alonsos exactly what they wanted: more traditional curtain panels for the windows and a wipe-clean nylon rug that is soft enough for the kids to play on. The most expensive part of the project was replacing the tile floor, but Adam says it was worth every penny. "It looks like it is authentic to our home," he says, "and the changes gave us two rooms we never previously utilized."

ACTUAL COST $40,000

BEFORE THE MAKEOVER

"By making the library built-in surround the sofa, the designers were able to maximize seating and comfort," homeowner Jen Alonso explains.

SALVAGED TILES

To make new floor tiles look like an original part of an older home or to give a new home an instant lived-in look, use either old salvaged tiles or tiles that have been distressed by the manufacturer to create an aged appearance. Old tiles can be purchased from architectural salvage dealers and antiques shops that specialize in architectural salvage. The plain floor tiles on the floor-level hearth *right* were originally salvaged from French churches and monasteries. The hand-painted decorative tiles are new Italian tiles that have been purposely distressed to look old. Because both tile types are handmade and irregular in size and thickness, a seasoned installer is recommended so that he or she can install the floor as flat as possible. Larger grout joints may also be necessary to make up for the variations in tile size.

IS IT OLD OR NEW? Dentil molding on the new built-in that surrounds the sofa *far right* matches the existing mantel. Corner shelves are stripped, sanded, and refinished to match the new wood. The new floral rug looks like it has always been a part of the decor in the living room, as do the muted colors and classic furnishings.

BEFORE THE MAKEOVER

BEFORE THE MAKEOVER

1 ROOM
3 WAYS

designers' challenge

pretty & pet-friendly

Matt and Diana McCutchen asked three designers to dress their basic bedroom and bath in both classic and pet-practical attire—with a budget of $20,000.

BEFORE THE MAKEOVER

DESIGNER DIANE KOLESAR, ETHAN ALLEN

DOGGY DUO. "Matt and Diana McCutchen have two large black Labrador retrievers, and their furnishings and fabrics need to be durable enough to stand up to paw prints and dog hair," Diane says. In her plan the focal point of the bedroom is a classic wooden sleigh bed that snuggles between existing windows. A silklike burgundy print duvet cover is fashioned from an easy-care polyester fabric and is accented by throw pillows in matching silks and coordinating trims. A washable burgundy throw tossed at the bottom of the bed protects the duvet from claw marks and provides a spot for one of the dogs to lie. On the far side of the bed, a round library table complements the couple's existing nightstand. Next to the table, a large custom dog bed disguises hair and complements the decor of the room.

VINTAGE SURROUND. To update the look of the fireplace, Diane suggests a custom-made surround of vintage moldings to tie it to the existing architectural features of the home. A round framed mirror above the mantel makes the area a secondary focal point.

READING ROOM. On the opposite side of the room, a new reading chair provides a spot to relax. Adjacent to the chair, a Bombay chest increases storage and complements the design of the existing armoire.

SWAGS AND CASCADES. All four small windows in the bedroom are treated with a swag, a cascade, and light-controlling wooden blinds. The larger window receives a secondary peaked swag. Similar window treatments adorn the windows in the master bath. Walls throughout both rooms are painted in a warm buff color. An Oriental area rug defines the seating area and ties together all the colors in the room.

SIMPLE SOLUTIONS. Reproduction fixtures, hardware, towel bars, and a candelabra give the basic bath a custom look for an affordable price. Baskets and rugs bring in welcome texture.

"My number one goal is to make my clients happy—to give them maximum impact for the dollars they're spending." DIANE KOLESAR

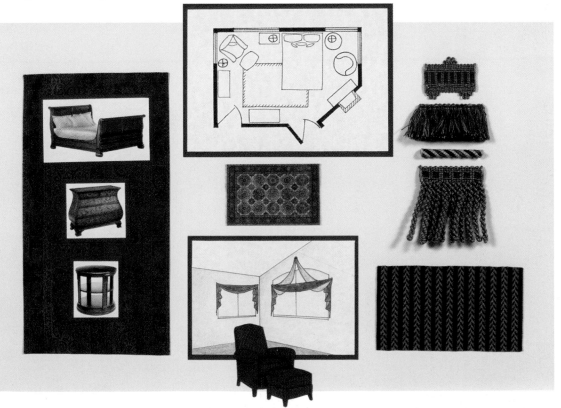

DESIGNER ERIC GUENTHER, GLABMAN'S FURNITURE AND INTERIOR DESIGN

VISUAL DIVIDE. Eric's layout draws attention to the architectural features of the bedroom by dividing the room into two sections: one under the existing low ceiling on the fireplace side and the other under the vaulted ceiling on the window side. Neutral tone-on-tone bedding is accented with colorful pillows.

PERFECT VIEW. The bed is angled from the corner to provide a direct view of the opposing fireplace. "The new sleigh bed is very dramatic, and I thought it was important to place it in the window section under the ceiling fan," Eric says. The armoire moves between the windows on the far wall of the suite so that it can be viewed from the entrance to the room.

HIS-AND-HERS SEATING. Granting the couple's request for a seating area, Eric has placed a chaise lounge, reading chair, table, and storage pedestal near the fireplace. Both the chaise and the reading chair are covered in a neutral-color print that coordinates with the bedding. Throw pillows introduce more texture and color. In front of the chaise, an antique reproduction rug ties all the colors in the room together.

SIMPLE WINDOW DRESSINGS. Roman shades begin at the ceiling line to make each window seem larger with one exception: On the arch-top window, the shade is cut to provide a peek of the rounded top.

COORDINATING WALLS. A paint color that is slightly warmer than the existing carpet dresses up the bedroom walls and draws attention to the moldings. A darker shade of the same color adds richness to the bathroom walls.

VANITY MAKEOVER. The bath cabinets are painted to create a distressed look and are adorned with reproduction hardware to complement the bedroom redesign.

"For a design to look and feel cohesive, there needs to be a marriage of at least two elements: the client's design aesthetic and the existing architecture." ERIC GUENTHER

3

DESIGNER JANIE BOWERS ALLIED ASID, JANIE BOWERS INTERIOR DESIGN

VISUAL LIFT. "The challenge of the McCutchen residence is to utilize the high ceilings and gorgeous soffits to create more visual space in the room," Janie says. To accomplish the goal, the walls are painted a soft taupe, and the soffit interior is highlighted with a richer golden tone. The moldings are accentuated with a lustrous cream-color paint.

HISTORICAL DESIGN. Furnishing selections have a romantic Renaissance feel. A large traditionally styled bed with a tall headboard and matching footboard serves as the focal point of the room. The bed is centered between two windows. A golden-and-red accent table serves as a nightstand on one side of the bed and complements the style of the existing nightstand on the other side. Matching beaded reading lamps top each bedside table.

CANINE COMPLEMENT. Fabrics throughout the suite are canine-friendly washable silks and chenilles. Janie also offers the dogs a handmade chairlike bed and creates a new fireplace design with moldings that complement the existing marble.

A rattan reading chair opposite the fireplace is accented by red and golden fabrics that coordinate with the dog bed. Next to the chair, a wall-hung sunburst mirror accents a new storage armoire.

CLASSIC PANELS. The windows are framed with simple floor-to-ceiling silk drapery panels.

BATH PLAN. For the bathroom Janie suggests new cabinetry hardware and fixtures made from either hand-hammered copper or pewter. The existing bath soffit is painted deep red to draw attention to the architectural feature. Below the soffit a small Japanese chair provides a resting spot.

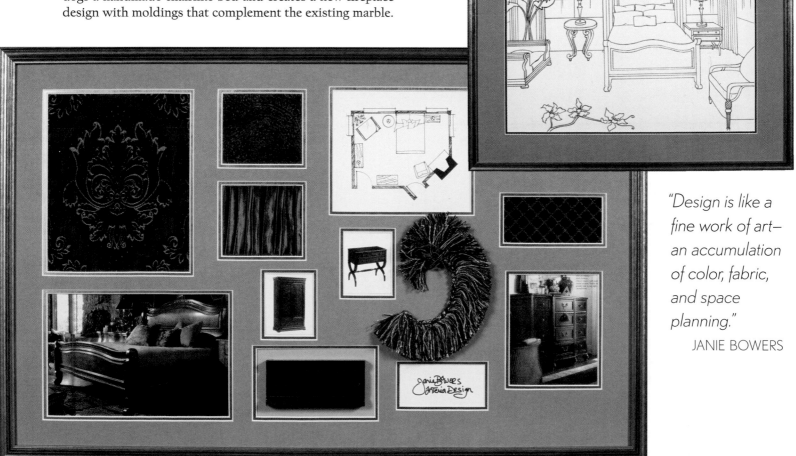

"Design is like a fine work of art— an accumulation of color, fabric, and space planning."

JANIE BOWERS

BEFORE THE MAKEOVER

BEFORE THE MAKEOVER

"Diane's presentation really captured the look we were after," homeowner Matt McCutchen says. Her suite design achieves the blend of elegance, warmth, and casual comfort the couple desired.

WHAT MAKES THIS PLAN WORK? Diane's plan addresses all the McCutchens' requests and complements the colors and styles the couple chose for the rest of their new home. A custom dog bed fashioned from antique furniture pieces and a mantel made from old architectural salvage *left* bring a sense of history into the new suite.

HOW CAN YOU GET THE LOOK? To create a similar look in your home, choose a dominant hue, such as the rich burgundy the McCutchens chose, and scatter the color throughout your room. "Color repetition keeps the eye moving and weaves spaces together," Diane explains. Use color on walls and floors as well as furnishings. Punctuate your design with accent colors in spots where you want the eye to linger, such as at the head of the bed or on the top of the fireplace mantel. Use patterns to visually link window dressings and upholstery and give the design a cohesive look.

DID THE DESIGNER MEET THE BUDGET? Remote-control blinds were more expensive than those suggested in the original plan, but they enable the McCutchens to alter the level of light and privacy in the room at the touch of a button. Hardware and fixtures in the bath were also upgraded. **ACTUAL COST** $26,000

"The new fireplace surround is made from salvaged moldings that complement the style of the traditional furnishings," designer Diane Kolesar says. "Simple custom touches like this give a room a very personal look."

PET SOLUTIONS

Providing pets with their own beds keeps wet paws and pet hair off the family furniture. Launder pet bedding frequently to keep dirt and hair under control. Frequent vacuuming of carpet and upholstered furnishings also helps prevent dust and hair from embedding in the fibers. Before vacuuming upholstery, check for loose buttons and threads; then vacuum over the fabric using a soft brush attachment. If the fabric has a nap (such as velvet or corduroy), vacuum in the direction of the nap, then run a dry towel over the fabric to smooth out vacuum lines. To remove pet hair from bed linens, use a handheld clothes lint remover or place the item in your dryer with an antistatic dryer sheet. Run the dryer on low heat for 20 to 30 minutes. Clean the lint trap after each load.

PERSONAL TOUCHES. Once cold and impersonal, the McCutchens' bedroom and bath now feel warm and welcoming. Antique-look area rugs brighten the original flooring in the bedroom *above left* and in the bath *opposite*. A cushy, classically styled chair and ottoman *above right* bring put-up-your-feet comfort to a corner of the bedroom. Even the dog bed *left* looks inviting—it's made from an old chair back and tabletop.

1 ROOM 3 WAYS

designers'challenge

classic&casual

BEFORE THE MAKEOVER

Brothers Craig and Darren Kaplan challenged designers to redecorate the great-room in their restored seaside bungalow on a budget of $20,000.

DESIGNER BRIGETTE BOYD ALLIED ASID, BRIGETTE BOYD INTERIORS

CASUAL ELEGANCE. "My vision for the Kaplan project is to make a space that is comfortable, casual, and quietly elegant," Brigette says. To make the living room feel inviting, she suggests a sofa and love seat in warm camel colors and a distressed leather chair that swivels to provide a view of the adjoining dining room.

VIBRANT RED ACCENTS. Red throw pillows and red motifs on the living room rug tie the design to the existing red walls. A coffee table and two complementary side tables serve as landing spots for snacks.

MANTEL MAKEOVER. To give the mantel more presence, the existing horizontal beam is eliminated and the bookshelves are enclosed; frosted-glass doors matching the style of the divided-light windows above the shelves keep audiovisual equipment under wraps. The bricks of the surround are glazed white to create a gracefully aged look.

FLEXIBLE DINING. In the adjacent dining room, a round dining table has two leaves that can comfortably accommodate up to 10 people. Wooden chairs are stained in a slightly darker shade than the table to give the appearance that the chairs were added over time. An area rug in a style and with colors similar to the rug in the living room further defines the space. A small buffet accommodates dinner service; a freestanding étagère provides a spot for displaying china.

SIMPLE SHADES. Throughout the space Roman shades mounted inside the window casings control light and heat, and show off the restored woodwork, which is painted white.

"What makes a room complete is color, line, and unity. When those are working together beautifully, you have a complete project." BRIGETTE BOYD

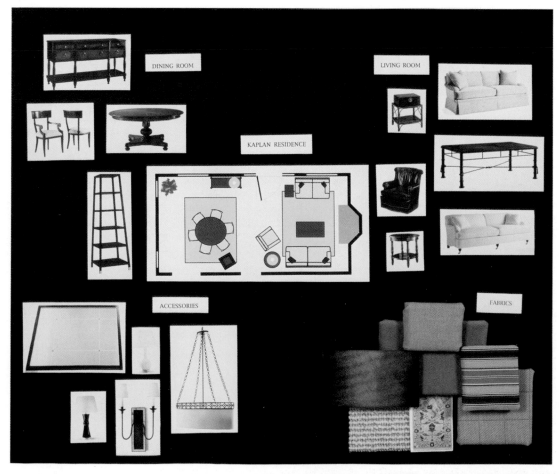

DINING ROOM

LIVING ROOM

KAPLAN RESIDENCE

ACCESSORIES

FABRICS

2

DESIGNER SUE GORMAN, SUE GORMAN INTERIOR DESIGNS

ACCOMMODATING LAYOUT. "The Kaplans' house needs to be comfortable enough for two, but also adaptable enough to accommodate large gatherings of family and friends," Sue says. Simple Craftsman-style furnishings perfectly suit the styling of the restored bungalow.

PAST PERFECT. The dining area is anchored with a custommade square area rug in wheat and red tones to complement the existing crimson walls. A reproduction Craftsman-style table and chairs provide seating for as many as eight. Stained-glass panels, another detail common in Craftsmanstyle homes, increase privacy in the front windows of the room. The dining room windows feature light-filtering pleated shades and fabric drapery panels.

AMPLE SEATING. A rug similar to the one in the dining room defines the seating area in the living room. A sectional sofa and a leather recliner provide flexible seating

for guests. The dining chairs can also be moved into the living area for "game-day" gatherings. New fireplace built-ins feature glass-front Craftsman-era styling seen elsewhere in the restored bungalow.

"WOW" EFFECT. "One of the things I like to do when I design a home is to create a 'wow' when you first walk in the door. The Kaplans' 'wow' is a grandfather clock placed against the wall opposite the door," Sue says.

"A designer really needs to push the envelope for clients beyond what they would do for themselves; otherwise, why do they need me?"

SUE GORMAN

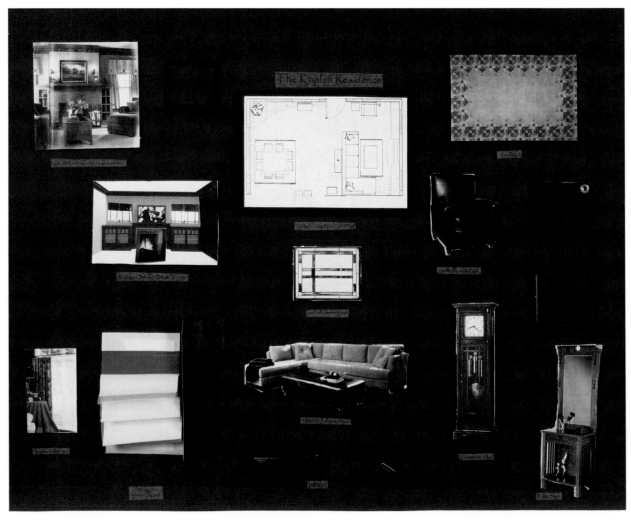

3

DESIGNER KELLY J. KELTER ALLIED ASID, DETAILS DESIGN

COZY COMFORT. "I want to create a comfy and cozy environment that is in keeping with the original style of the cottage," Kelly says.

FOCAL-POINT FIREPLACE. To give the fireplace in the living area more prominence, Kelly suggests refacing the tired bricks with natural stone tiles. Building the fireplace out and moving the existing sconces a few inches provides enough space for new built-in cabinets that replicate the style of the existing built-in cabinets in the dining room.

RELAXED ENTERTAINING. An L-shape sectional sofa combines with a reclining chair for seating that's suitable for relaxing alone or entertaining. A leather ottoman doubles as a sofa table and provides hidden storage for magazines and remote controls. A nearby stacking tray table enables the homeowners to enjoy refreshments in front of the television. A table placed behind the sofa provides display space and a spot for serving food and drinks.

COLORFUL DINING. A decorative stained-glass panel adorns the wall above the existing built-ins in the dining room and draws attention to the original cabinets. A red table runner adds drama and ties the tabletop to the painted walls. Sheer window treatments combine with classic drapery panels that can be drawn shut when privacy is desired.

COLOR OPTIONS. Kelly offers three color scheme options so that the owners can choose the fabrics they like best without having to make individual fabric selections. Photos and artwork from the owners' travels are enlarged and framed to create a personalized "art wall."

LIGHT CONTROL. Existing sconces, chandeliers, and recessed lights work in conjunction with new dimmer switches to control ambient and mood lighting.

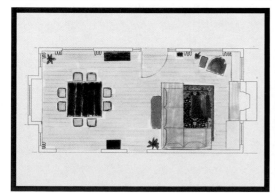

KAPLAN RESIDENCE

"Lighting can make or break a room. When you combine the correct lighting with a coordinated design that complements the rest of the house, you know you have achieved decorating success." KELLY J. KELTER

Designer Kelly Kelter's focal-point fireplace sold brothers Craig and Darren Kaplan on her design.

WHAT MAKES THIS PLAN WORK? Kelly's cozy and eclectic design matches the brothers' easy-going personalities and complements the styling of the cottage.

HOW CAN YOU GET THE LOOK? "Repeating design details in open and adjacent rooms provides visual continuity and creates a very personal look," Kelly explains. When decorating your home, repeat details and use different shades of the same colors to connect your spaces. For example in the Kaplans' home, floor-to-ceiling camel-color silk panel draperies and decorative walls sconces are used throughout the adjoining areas. Also personalize rooms with photographs and mementos that offer guests a glimpse of your personality, as Kelly did by hanging the brothers' travel photos. To maximize display space without creating a cluttered appearance, take advantage of often-wasted space by choosing sofa and occasional tables that have two or more display shelves as shown *left*. Finally select furnishings and accessories that match your lifestyle. In the Kaplans' home, a square, upholstered ottoman provides a spot where they can put up their feet and place a bowl of chips; the leather fabric wipes clean with a damp cloth. A new ceiling fan installed in the living area keeps air circulating and cuts down on summer cooling costs. "It's these little additions that truly make a house a home," Darren Kaplan says.

DID THE DESIGNER MEET THE BUDGET? Careful editing of furnishing selections before presenting them to the Kaplans enabled Kelly to meet the budget.

ACTUAL COST $20,000

BEFORE THE MAKEOVER

"When my brother and I found this neglected beachside cottage, we knew we could restore it to its original condition, but we needed a professional designer to help us pull the furnishings and all the accessories together," Darren Kaplan says.

MADE TO ORDER. Pale limestone tiles imported from Portugal shown on *page 76* update the fireplace surround and provide welcome contrast between the existing red walls and the warm oak floors. A faux "smoke chamber" above the mantel surrounds the flat-screen plasma TV and melds the TV into the overall design of the fireplace. Personal travel pictures in matching frames *above* adorn the wall above the L of the sectional sofa. Existing open shelves *opposite* are updated with flat-panel glass doors that complement the style of other built-ins. The chest by the front door *left* provides storage and display space.

"We started out with very few furnishings, and what we did have belonged in a fraternity house," Craig Kaplan says.

CHOOSE YOUR FOCUS

Every gathering area needs a focal point—an anchor around which your design revolves. If your living room has a natural architectural focus, such as a fireplace, built-ins, or a great view, position seating around it. If not create your own focal point with a grouping of colorful prints, a large decorative mirror hung above a console table, or a large-scale furnishing such as the built-in hutch *above* and *right*. A focal point gives the eye a starting point from which it can take in the entire room with ease.

1 ROOM
3 WAYS

designers'challenge family living&dining

the choices

With a budget of $25,000, Marc and Cindy Miller asked three designers to restyle their living and dining rooms into family-friendly gathering spaces.

BEFORE THE MAKEOVER

DESIGNER ANNIE SPECK ASID, ANNIE SPECK INTERIOR DESIGNS

OPEN ROOMS. "Cindy and Marc Miller's living and dining rooms are open to one another, so they need to look good and work well together," Annie says. "My design vision is to create a feeling of cozy and casual elegance." Walls throughout the space are washed in pale golden yellows. Tone-on-tone botanical-print curtain panels accent existing blinds.

AMPLE SEATING. In the living room a wood floor and a large sisal area rug replace existing carpet. Because the space is relatively large, the conversation area is defined by the border of the rug and includes a golden-yellow chenille sofa and three side chairs with patterned upholstery. The arrangement provides comfortable seating for up to eight people. A large square cocktail table offers space for playing board games and cards. New lamps placed on a variety of occasional tables supply reading and accent lighting. A new oil painting above the existing piano introduces more color and provides a decorative focal point for the living room.

ENTRY FOCAL POINT. In the long open entryway, Annie suggests an antique French chest with a distressed finish to break up the space and provide storage for keys and whatnot.

DOUBLE-DUTY BUFFET. A reproduction Portuguese trestle table extends to more than 8 feet to accommodate as many as 10 diners in the adjacent dining room. An Oriental wool rug warms the existing terra-cotta tile floor. English-style upholstered chairs provide comfortable and elegant seating. A long, custom-made buffet doubles as a workstation for the Millers' two school-age children; mirrored doors on each end of the buffet disguise computer monitors. The chandelier is hung high enough to adequately light the workstation and the tabletop.

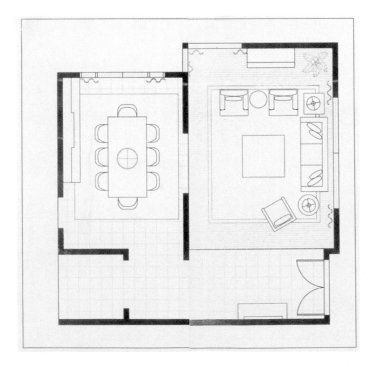

"A good design improves the quality of life, not only with the aesthetics but also with how the environment functions." ANNIE SPECK

2 DESIGNER LINDA LANSFORD, LINDA LANSFORD INTERIOR DESIGN

CLASSIC AND PRACTICAL. Linda's design combines classic styles with modern practicality. In the entryway a narrow trestle table offers a spot for displaying decorative collectibles as well as dropping car keys and mail. Below the table two small leather-covered ottomans open up to yield storage space or can be pulled into the adjacent living area for extra seating.

SEATING FOR SIX. In the living room a chenille sofa and love seat are offset by a comfy zebra-print side chair. Floral-print draperies with terra-cotta-color accents and a coordinating trim adorn the windows. Accent pillows are made from the same signature fabric as the draperies. A bamboo cocktail table with cut corners echoes the shape of the original tray ceiling in the dining room. The existing plush, pale camel-color carpet remains.

FULL-WALL WORK CENTER. Terra-cotta-color paint accents the tray ceiling in the dining room. A new 7-foot-long trestle table accommodates up to eight diners. Behind the dining table a library wall doubles as work space for the children. The built-in storage wall features dual desks, open shelves, and retractable doors that disguise computer monitors. "These changes make underutilized rooms into inviting gathering spaces that the Millers can look forward to using everyday," Linda says.

"Interior design has to be functional as well as beautiful. If a room doesn't work for the people who are using it, then it's really not a good room."

LINDA LANSFORD

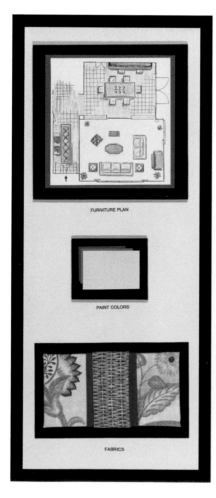

FURNITURE PLAN

PAINT COLORS

FABRICS

LIVING ROOM

DINING ROOM

LIVING ROOM

ENTRY

DINING ROOM

3

DESIGNER SALLY KETTERER ALLIED ASID, CID, IDS, SALLY KETTERER INTERIORS

BEAUTY AND DURABILITY. Warm colors, custom finishes, and durable fabrics are the mainstays of Sally's design.

TALLER WALL. The existing half-wall between the dining room and living area is raised to 8 feet to allow for a pair of wooden bookcases on the living room side. The bookcases offset the existing step-up entrance of the dining room.

MATCHING FABRIC SEATING. Beyond the bookcases a soft green chenille love seat and sofa combine with two side chairs with matching upholstery to furnish seating for up to eight people. Toss pillows are made from a contemporary leaf- and animal-print fabric. A large, square wooden cocktail table provides a spot for playing games and displaying collectibles, while a pair of complementary occasional tables holds reading lamps and decorative accessories. Large potted trees bring life into the exterior corners of the room. The existing plush, pale camel-color carpet remains.

SIMPLY FURNISHED ENTRANCE. A sofa table with two storage drawers fits against the wall near the entrance of the home and supplies a landing spot for mail and keys.

INDIVIDUAL WORKSTATIONS. In the dining room two custom armoires with a cinnamon-tone stain are placed on opposite walls and serve as individual workstations for the kids. A smaller wood-tone hutch provides buffet service. To bring in more color, earthy cinnamon-color paint coats one wall of the dining room and accents the inside of the double front doors in the entryway.

"The key to good design is a good plan. If you stay on track with your plan, you will have a beautiful outcome." SALLY KETTERER

"It was a difficult decision for us because we knew all three of the designs would look great in the space, but in the end we chose Annie," homeowner Marc Miller says.

WHAT MAKES THIS PLAN WORK? "We loved Annie's plan for the kids' work space, making it both beautiful and purposeful," Cindy says. "It looks like a traditional buffet but is actually an incredibly functional work center." The trestle-style table is durable enough to use as an extra work surface and elegant enough for gourmet dining. Because they are fully upholstered, the dining chairs are comfortable enough to move into the living room to accommodate overflow seating. Seating for eight or more people in both the living room and the dining room enables the family to entertain a crowd or spread out and spend quality time together.

HOW CAN YOU GET THE LOOK? If your room has a high or vaulted ceiling, visually lower it by painting the walls a warm or vibrant color as shown *left*. Choose a hue found in existing furnishings or woodwork.

Here soft golden-yellow color-washed walls bring out the richness of the various woods used throughout the rooms. Instead of wall-to-wall carpet, opt for wooden floors. (Or, to reduce costs, install a 2-foot-wide wood-plank border around the perimeter of the room and lay carpeting in the middle.) Bring additional color into the room with throw pillows and area rugs. The floral-print dining room rug shown on *page 90* brings out the red in the existing earthy terra-cotta tiles and can withstand spills.

BEFORE THE MAKEOVER

BEFORE THE MAKEOVER

DID THE DESIGNER MEET THE BUDGET? Frugal shopping at several design sources enabled Annie to complete the room on time and on budget.

ACTUAL COST $25,000

"The rooms still feel open and airy, but they have a new warmth and a richness that encourages gathering and togetherness," designer Annie Speck explains.

COHESIVE DESIGN. Oak floors warm the living room *above* and complement the existing tiles in the dining room and entryway *left*. Throw pillows *above left* and *opposite* introduce color and texture to the living room. Golden accents—on the mirror in the entry and on the picture frame in the living room—draw out the golden hues in the drapery panels and in the color-washed walls.

"The spaces are so much more pulled together," homeowner Cindy Miller says. "We find ourselves spending a lot more time in these two rooms."

PERSONAL BEST

The most successful interiors match your personality and the character of your home. These basic principles of design can help make your interiors shine.

● RESPECT THE ARCHITECTURE OF YOUR HOME. If you live in a Craftsman-style cottage, for example, choose an interior design that pays homage to the simple lines and casual elegance typical of the style. If, on the other hand, you're redoing a 100-year-old Victorian home, choose a few furniture pieces—antique or reproduction—that look as old and ornate as the house.

● TAKE YOUR TIME. Good design takes time, so mixing is a must. The most eye-appealing designs look as though they've been completed over a long period of time rather than pulled together from one singular source. In the Millers' dining room *right* and *opposite,* wood tones complement one another but don't match exactly.

● SHARE YOUR PASSIONS. If you love flow blue china or architectural salvage, show it off in open shelves or glass-front cupboards. Sharing what you love offers a piece of your personality to friends and family and makes your home feel warm and welcoming.

● CHOOSE FURNISHINGS AND SURFACES THAT SUIT YOUR LIFESTYLE. There is nothing more uncomfortable than a room filled with furnishings no one is allowed to sit on— unless it is a formal entertaining space. Choose furniture upholstery that matches the activities that occur in that particular room. For instance if your children and pets use your living room as play central, select washable, durable fabrics that stand up to wear and cover the floor with materials that withstand spills and splashes. It will make life easier by reducing cleanup chores and stress.

BEFORE THE MAKEOVER.

FUNCTIONAL AND COMFORTABLE. The areas in which we dine and work at home need to be functional, but that doesn't mean they can't be stylish too. The dining room *opposite* and homework nook *above* feature a soothing color palette, comfortable chairs, and personal collections that complement the living room. When the work is done, doors conceal the workstations, seamlessly blending the office into the dining room.

1 ROOM
3 WAYS

designers'challenge lofty expectations

Scott Damman asked three designers to transform his industrial loft into a contemporary space that accommodates entertaining, relaxing, and daily living—all on a budget of $40,000.

BEFORE THE MAKEOVER

DESIGNER TERRI MAIN ALLIED ASID, MAIN DESIGN INNOVATIONS

CUSTOM FURNISHINGS. "This project is about city living and preserving the history inherent in a loft space, as well as addressing Scott Damman's needs," Terri says. Her innovative plan uses custom furniture pieces made by local artisans to bring more comfort into the industrial space.

DOLLOPS OF COLOR. Neutral creams and soft grays lighten the walls throughout the space; cool gray solar reflector film covers the windows to control heat and light. Shots of vibrant reds, sunny yellows, deep blues, and celery greens on furnishings and fabrics brighten the entire space.

MEDIA MOGUL. The media room remains in its current location, but two new contemporary sofas and a custom-made mahogany entertainment center make the space look and feel more comfortable. A one-of-a-kind slate cocktail table sits between the sofas. Overhead, three pear-shape bubble lamps enhance natural lighting.

FLEXIBLE DINING. The dining area expands to include two tables on coasters so that Scott can easily call them into action for larger gatherings. A serving cart—stationed between the tables—accommodates hors d'oeuvres and buffet service. Above the tables, handblown glass fixtures attach to dimmer switches to provide mood lighting. Chaise lounges stand at the ready to offer a spot for relaxing after dinner.

PARTY PLATFORM. Beyond the dining center, an elevated platform, painted in soft grays and blues, accommodates more than two dozen guests. Ottomanlike seating and cube-shape parsons tables create a unique gathering space.

FLOORPLAN

"I specialize in cutting-edge contemporary, classic modern, and Art Deco styles. My approach as a designer is respect for the architecture, first and foremost." TERRI MAIN

2

DESIGNER BARBI KRASS ALLIED ASID, COLORWORKS STUDIO

ENTERTAINMENT DECK. "When designing a loft space, you have to be careful to preserve the industrial flavor of the space and make sure that all the areas work together both visually and functionally," Barbi says. The focal point of her plan is an entertainment deck. "We raised the deck to just below window height so that guests have a great view of the city," she explains. The deck is large enough to accommodate 25 people.

PRACTICAL SEATING. Three taupe-color faux-suede sectionals combine with cushioned walnut side chairs to provide ample seating on the raised platform. A rolling table and bar can be moved between the deck and the existing dining area to make serving multiple guests easier. Adjacent to the entertainment deck, a smaller seating area is furnished with a small table and retro shag carpet for more intimate gatherings and daily dining. Beyond the round table, a table for 20 is appropriate for larger gatherings. Additional walnut chairs can be moved between the areas to accommodate varying numbers of guests.

TV VIEWING. The TV room is fitted with 8-foot-high partial walls, creating a denlike feel. A geometric-print area rug, a dusty blue-color faux-suede sofa, and a cushy ottoman create a practical and comfortable viewing area. A luxurious leather chair and a second ottoman provide additional seating. An entertainment center constructed of bronze metal houses all the media equipment.

SHADED WINDOWS. To control heat and glare typically associated with a space that has multiple windows, three solar shades per window are installed. Contemporary streetlights mounted on the existing structural columns provide dramatic yet functional ambient lighting.

"I like to approach design with an open mind, a sense of humor, and an eye for longevity. My goal is for the owner to come back to me in a number of years, and say 'I still love the room; let's do another one.'"

BARBI KRASS

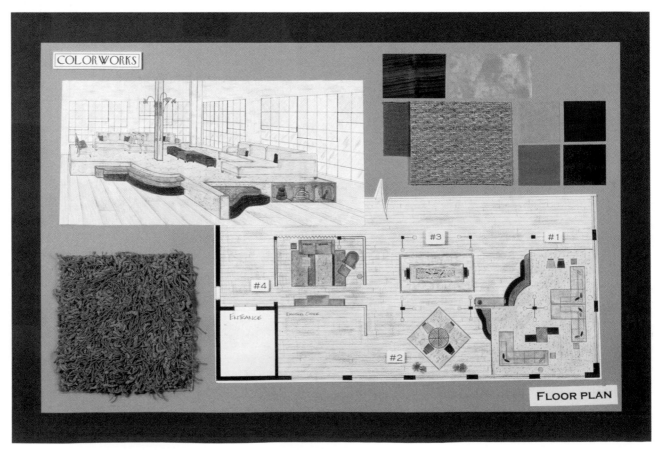

COLORWORKS

#3 #1

#4

#2

ENTRANCE

FLOOR PLAN

3

DESIGNER ELLEN PREMTAJ, ELLE INTERIORS

SEPARATE YET OPEN. "The intriguing part of this design is defining all of the spaces but still keeping it as one cohesive environment," Ellen says.

VISUAL DIVIDE. A 10-foot-high privacy screen separates the media center from the remainder of the loft. An L-shape sofa combines with a custom ottoman to seat more than a dozen guests. Commercial carpet tiles in a variety of colors warm the floor.

PILLARED DINING. Six existing structural pillars define the dining area. A long dining table accommodates up to 14 people. Stackable steel chairs with molded wood seats easily tuck away when not in use. Halogen pendant light fixtures illuminate the tabletop.

HIGH STYLE. A 1-foot-high L-shape platform defines the living area. Easy-care woven vinyl covers the platform, ushering in additional color and texture. A large sectional sofa is made from a variety of pieces to seat as many as 20 guests. Hollow cube tables with solid-surface tops provide both storage space and a landing spot for food and drinks.

"What makes a room complete is addressing all the elements in the space and keeping it clean, elegant, and timeless." ELLEN PREMTAJ

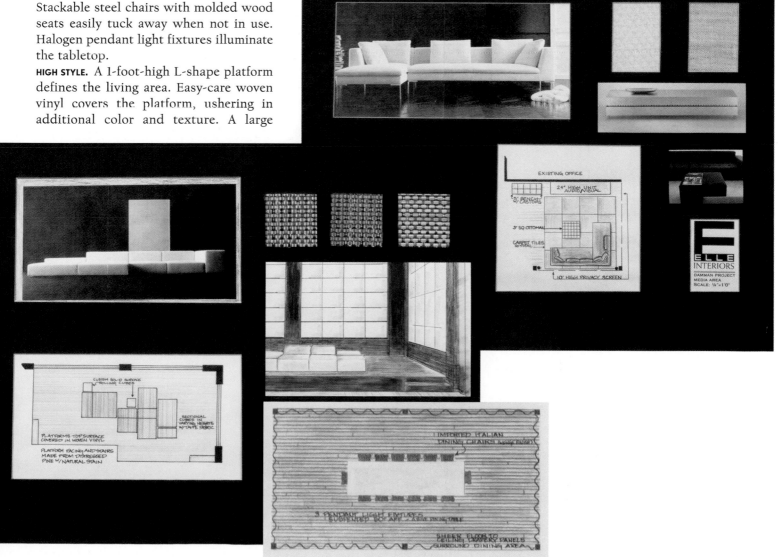

2 "Barbi Krass put together the most comprehensive plan and the best bang for the buck that was going to suit my needs," loft owner Scott Damman says.

WHAT MAKES THIS PLAN WORK? A raised platform *opposite* combines with existing pillars to visually define each new gathering space. A ramp leading to the platform *above* enables the rolling bar and other mobile furnishings to glide between levels. Corrugated-steel partitions shown on *page 99*—which Scott suggested—are used in place of the permanent partial walls originally planned by Barbi. These dividers provide layout flexibility because they can be reconfigured to accommodate various room layouts and amounts of guests. When not being used for entertaining, the 14-foot-long dining table *above right* also serves as a display space for collectibles. The poured-concrete legs, another plan modification, complement the concrete countertops in the kitchen.

HOW CAN YOU GET THE LOOK? When remodeling or redecorating a space with industrial roots, choose materials and furnishings that pay homage to that history. In this space steel, wood, and brick combine with softer fabrics and materials to create a home that is comfortable yet complementary to the architectural style of the loft. If you entertain on a grand scale as Scott does, choose flexible furnishings—for instance those on wheels—that you can move to meet the needs of each event.

DID THE DESIGNER MEET THE BUDGET? To ensure the budget was met, Barbi carefully planned and priced out each phase of the project so that there were no surprises.

ACTUAL COST $40,000

"Nearly all the furnishings in this space are custom," designer Barbi Krass explains. "Most are on a grand scale to complement the massive proportions of the loft space."

RETRO OR CONTEMPORARY?

Although the 1950s are often viewed as a simpler time, some of the furniture designs were actually quite sophisticated and are the inspiration behind many of the furnishings in this loft, which Colorworks Studio created. That "back to the future" time, known as the Mid-Century Modern period, lasted from 1947 to 1957. It marked the beginning of funky design, with furniture and accessories made from newly developed materials such as fiberglass, acrylic, foam rubber, and molded plywood. Furniture of the period is ultracreative with seats that are slung low to the ground and conform to the shape of the body. Although originally sporting chrome and blond woods, today's pieces take on a studier, more industrial look with heavier metals and warmer woods, as seen in the pieces in this loft. The back-to-back sofas *opposite far right* are reminiscent of Hollywood-style divans that can be seen on the set of many a black and white television show.

ACCESSIBLE DESIGN

Although Scott Damman's loft was not specifically designed with accessibility in mind, it has some great features that enable friends and family members of all ages and abilities to feel comfortable and welcome. Wide walkways, elevator access to the loft, and a single-story design make Scott's home comfortable for both wheelchairs and walkers. A ramp leading to the party platform provides access for a rolling bar and is an alternative to stairs.

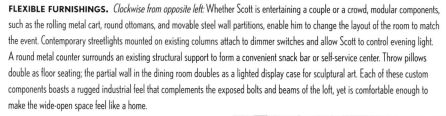

FLEXIBLE FURNISHINGS. *Clockwise from opposite left:* Whether Scott is entertaining a couple or a crowd, modular components, such as the rolling metal cart, round ottomans, and movable steel wall partitions, enable him to change the layout of the room to match the event. Contemporary streetlights mounted on existing columns attach to dimmer switches and allow Scott to control evening light. A round metal counter surrounds an existing structural support to form a convenient snack bar or self-service center. Throw pillows double as floor seating; the partial wall in the dining room doubles as a lighted display case for sculptural art. Each of these custom components boasts a rugged industrial feel that complements the exposed bolts and beams of the loft, yet is comfortable enough to make the wide-open space feel like a home.

When remodeling your living space, consider widening doorways and hallways to a minimum of 4 feet and make entrances and exits level to the ground—you'll appreciate the comfort as much as the next person. (To prevent water from seeping in the doors at a level entrance, extend overhangs a minimum of 3 feet.) Should a friend or family member ever break a leg or have surgery on a knee or a hip, they'll appreciate the comfortable access too. Similarly, being able to wheel a high chair, a rolling crib, or a baby stroller through the house reduces strain on your back and may alleviate the need to wake a sleeping baby. The following guidelines from the National Kitchen and Bath Association can also increase the accessibility in your home.

● DOOR SIZE. Plan for a clear door opening of 36 inches. Larger openings are difficult to open and close from a seated position, and narrower openings make it difficult, if not impossible, for a wheelchair to make it through.

● FLOOR SPACE. For a typical-size wheelchair to make a complete turnaround, you'll need to leave a circular area of clear floor space measuring 5 feet in diameter. Leave an area in front of the kitchen or bath sink that measures at least 30x48 inches. Toilets need a clear floor space that is 48 inches square. Bathtubs need a clear floor space of 60x60 inches in front of the tub.

● BATHING COMFORT. Shower stalls are easier to get in and out of than bathtubs. Choose a stall that measures at least 4 feet square with no curb or a very short one.

1 ROOM
3 WAYS

designers'challenge

remake by remodeling

The eight rooms showcased in this section go beyond simple surface makeovers. You'll see how moving doors and windows can increase functionality and open rooms to light and views. You'll learn what trials and tribulations come with tearing down a load-bearing wall and how to-the-studs renovations can make new rooms look like they've always been a part of your home.

1 ROOM
3 WAYS

designers'challenge vacation 24/7

Is it possible to make a dated A-frame cabin look and feel like a luxury live-in retreat on a $30,000 budget? That's the charge the Markgrafs gave three designers.

BEFORE THE MAKEOVER

DESIGNER ANNIE WALTON-TETER, STUDIO ANNIK

SURFACE SOLUTIONS. Annie's design plan instills an airy and spacious feeling in Mark and Yvonne Markgraf's A-frame cabin with neutral tones and smooth finishes. "What I found challenging about the Markgrafs' home is the fireplace," Annie says. "Because of all the cedar paneling, it's really quite dark." Cream-painted drywall replaces dark cedar paneling on the long fireplace chimney. Beige stone look-alike ceramic tiles cover the hearth, the surround, and the entryway floor. A heavily textured stain-resistant wool-blend carpet that adds comfort underfoot covers the floor of the living and dining spaces.

STORAGE CUBBIES. New natural maple built-ins turn a short cedar wall into an attractive audiovisual storage and display case. A cushy upholstered chair and an ottoman placed opposite the built-ins provide a spot for relaxing and listening to music.

FAMILY GATHERING. On the wall opposite the fire-place, a new slipcovered sofa provides wash-and-wear comfort for the young family of three. A large rectangular coffee table features a storage shelf underneath that helps keep clutter under control. A large framed mirror above the sofa reflects the opposing view and brings even more light into the space.

CHILD SAFETY. New stainless-steel fireplace doors visually tie the family room to the adjacent kitchen and make the wood-burning unit safer for the couple's daughter.

"My overall philosophy about design and approach is that less is more."

ANNIE WALTON-TETER

2

DESIGNER RON HUNT CID, HAVEN GROVE DESIGN GROUP, LLC

UNOBSTRUCTED VIEW. "What I'd like to create for the Markgrafs is a sense that nature is coming inside their home rather than that they are rooted in the middle of it and not able to visually experience it," Ron says. His plans call for a major realignment of both the exterior and interior spaces to capitalize on the view. The existing fireplace is removed to create a wall of glass that floods the room with daylight.

MORE GLASS. The old front door is removed and replaced with a large etched-glass fixed window panel that ushers in even more natural light. A glass entrance door near the new fireplace opens the great-room to the view. Pale green color-washed walls complement the woodland setting and maximize light reflection.

VISUAL DIVIDE. A combination of new carpet and the existing wood flooring separates the great-room into functional areas. Floor-to-ceiling custom cabinetry between the kitchen and the new entryway provides additional storage for audiovisual equipment and the couple's expansive album collection. As a bonus, the hutchlike unit also limits views of the food preparation area in the kitchen. A huge chandelier hung from the apex of the cabin fills the space with ambient light.

KINETIC GLOW. A new wood-burning stove is installed near an adjacent sidewall, making it visible from nearly every section of the great-room. Low-key yet comfortable furnishings include an easy-care sofa and two leather chairs. A central ottoman serves as either a footstool or a serving tray. The dining table is moved to provide room for a new display hutch for Yvonne's china.

EXPAND THE DESIGN BOUNDARIES. Outside, the porch railing is replaced with steps to further reduce visual obstructions. When the budget permits, a fire pit is suggested to enhance outdoor entertaining during cooler months.

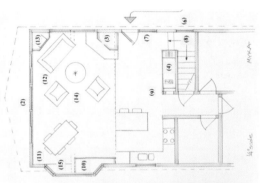

"The completion of a room in my eyes is lighting and greenery. They are the anchors that ground a design." RON HUNT

DESIGNER KIM SCHERZI, PORTA BELLA

OLD AND NEW. "The Markgrafs' A-frame cabin has potential. There is a lot that can be done to lighten and brighten the space," Kim says. Her eclectic plan mixes old-world Italian furniture with contemporary accent pieces and colors.

OPEN ENTRANCE. A cedar wall blocking the existing entry door is moved back 3 feet to open the area to more light and views. A new built-in entertainment center on the living room side of the shortened wall provides storage for audio-visual equipment. Albums and videos are tucked away in drawers, keeping clutter to a minimum.

BRIGHTER OUTLOOK. To lighten the great-room, the cedar chimney behind the existing fireplace is covered with drywall and painted a creamy white. A freestanding wood-burning stove located just in front of the drywall chimney replaces the built-in unit. A combination of chandeliers and pendant lights enhances natural lighting. White linen drapery panels provide privacy when desired. Underfoot, a wheat-color sisal rugs disguises spills and footprints, which is important for a young family that will be going in and out frequently.

FLEXIBLE SEATING. A sectionallike taupe-color chenille sofa flows around an existing structural beam and is joined by either two dark brown leather swivel chairs or a trio of ottomans. Throw pillows feature different fabrics on the front and back to create a new look for summer and winter.

DINING ROOM DO-OVER. A built-in china cabinet placed on the wall behind the dining table provides storage for dishware. The old wooden dining table is replaced by a clear acrylic glass table that can be extended to seat as many as eight.

"Design is all about researching what is available and putting together a plan that is both functional and comfortable." KIM SCHERZI

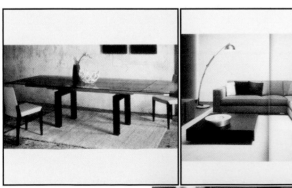

2

"Ron Hunt's plan included everything we asked for plus a few extra indulgences," homeowner Mark Markgraf says. "The project took a little longer than we thought—just over six months—but in the end, we got everything we wanted and we're very happy."

WHAT MAKES THIS PLAN WORK? Moving the fireplace and filling the A-frame's apex wall with glass maximizes the infiltration of both sunlight and views *opposite*. At the height of the A-frame, a massive chandelier lights the great-room when sunlight doesn't. Removing the old front door and replacing it with an art-glass window creates a sun-kissed landing at the bottom of the stairwell. The relocated entry door provides a more spacious and elegant entrance. Custom cabinetry visually separates the kitchen from the great-room and offers storage for a large collection of audiovisual equipment. Fresh drywall replaces a large portion of the dark cedar paneling. Leaf-pattern nylon carpet fits the cabin-in-the-woods theme and is virtually kid-proof. A variety of potted trees and tropical plants connects the interior to the outdoors.

HOW CAN YOU GET THE LOOK? To make every day feel like a vacation, you need to open your home to as much natural light and as many views as possible, Ron says. "Choose fabric and surfaces that not only complement the view, but that are also easy to care for. That way you can spend your free time playing instead of working." If possible he suggests angling seating to take full advantage of a pretty vista as he did in the arrangement *opposite*. The leather chair *right* wipes clean, and the patterned chenille sofa and ottoman disguise dirt.

DID THE DESIGNER MEET THE BUDGET? Ron's thorough remodeling plan enabled the couple to complete the remodeling on budget. Future enhancements are planned for outdoor living spaces.

ACTUAL COST $30,000

"A design is never complete until each accessory is in place," designer Ron Hunt says.

"A good designer takes what clients view as everyday annoyances and transforms them into functional focal points," designer Ron Hunt says.

GOODBYE BUDGET

Are your plans bigger than your budget? If so consider this advice: "When determining what it is you would really like from your remodeling, make a list that isn't bound by schedules or money, then think of ways you can accomplish the goals over time," says designer Ron Hunt. "My vision for the Markgrafs' home was actually much more than what you see. I gave them a five-year plan that they can accomplish as time and budget allow. It may sound cliché, but when it comes to problem-solving, you need to think outside the box."

BEFORE THE MAKEOVER

BEFORE THE MAKEOVER

LET THERE BE LIGHT. Shadowy corners, underlit work surfaces, and overpowering paneling made the Markgrafs' cabin feel dark and uninviting. Now pale-painted drywall brightens many of the walls *above right*, and a huge custom-made iron chandelier *above left* makes evenings nearly as bright as mornings. A new dining hutch complements the table, while the existing chairs are given a stylish and low-cost makeover with bright red slipcovers *opposite*.

1
ROOM
3
WAYS

designers'**challenge**

asianbath**oasis**

BEFORE THE MAKEOVER

Kim and Fred Chung asked designers to recast their bath into a spalike oasis where they can relax together each day—on a budget of $50,000.

ARCHITECTS MICHELLE KAUFMANN AIA, MK ARCHITECTURE & CAMILLE URBAN JOBE AIA, URBAN JOBE ARCHITECTURE

ROOM FOR TWO. "We'd like to take these 'passing ships in the night' and give them an inviting place to rendezvous," Michelle says of Kim and Fred Chung, professionals who work long hours and often travel for business in opposite directions. The architects suggest removing the wall between the bathroom and the laundry room to more than double the size of the master bath. The laundry area moves to an underused closet in a nearby hallway.

COMPARTMENTALIZED PLAN. The bath itself is divided into three functional areas. The first area contains a toilet compartment that houseguests can access. The second area encompasses two vanities on opposite walls, allowing Kim and Fred to use the sinks at the same time. The third area is a private space for the couple, which houses a soaking tub and an open shower—both large enough for two.

FENG SHUI AMBIENCE. The architectural team envisions a tranquil space closely tied to the nature-inspired elements found in luxurious spa retreats: the essence of water, fire, wood, earth, and metal. The "water" zone includes the shower and soaking tub. The "fire" wall behind the tub can be seen all the way to the bath entrance and features tumbled Italian stone and several display shelves that hold an array of candles. The "wood" element is represented in custom-made vanities. The "earth" connection comes from all the natural elements used in the bath, including the travertine countertops, floor, and shower surround as well as a bamboo planter near the entrance to the bath. Metal fixtures and faucets provide the final *feng shui* component.

FUNCTIONAL STORAGE. Storage features include wide medicine cabinets installed behind the vanity mirrors, recessed display niches on both sides of the two vanities, and deep drawers below the sinks that are fitted with compartmentalized storage bins.

"We look for the essence of a project—what should it feel like? how should it function?— to solve a design problem in a thoughtful way."

MICHELLE KAUFMANN

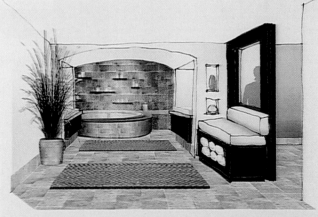

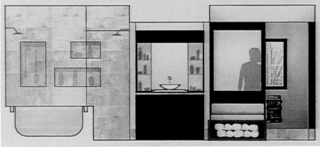

DESIGNER YVONNE LANE WONDER ALLIED ASID, YVONNE LANE INTERIOR LLC

TWICE THE SIZE. "My vision for the bath is a warm, inviting, and relaxing space that you look forward to entering each day," Yvonne says. As in Michelle and Camille's plan on *page 111*, the laundry area is annexed into the bath. A new laundry closet is added to a back hall.

HOTEL AMENITIES. Hotellike amenities include a curved double-sink vanity, a separate well-lit makeup vanity for Kim, a whirlpool tub, and a multiple-head shower that accommodates two.

SOFT COLORS. Earth tones and pale warm yellows create a sophisticated and tranquil ambience. Brushed-chrome fixtures are contemporary and easy to care for.

TIMELESS SURFACES. Travertine tiles in a playful pattern are proposed for the floor, while 12-inch-square ceramic tiles in earthy tones protect the inside corner walls of the shower; tempered glass covers the outer walls. Marble in a deep chocolate color tops the vanity. Custom cabinets feature flat-panel doors made from German Black Forest wood and furniture-style legs. A large custom-made mirror covers the wall behind the makeup vanity. A large linen closet, a medicine cabinet, and pullout shelves within each vanity base provide ample storage space.

"The most important element in the design of a room is determining how it is going to be used and then designing around that so that the room serves its purpose." YVONNE LANE WONDER

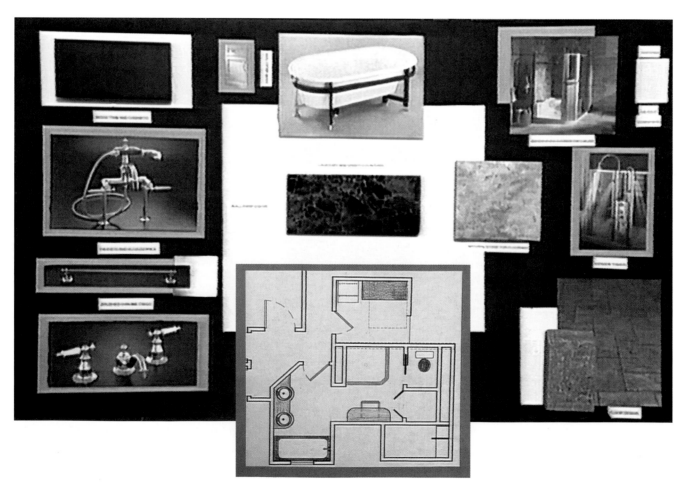

3

DESIGNER ALBERT CAREY ASID, NKBA, LAMPERTI ASSOCIATES

MORE FROM LESS. "My vision for the Chung bathroom is to create a serene retreat that feels separate and distinct from the rest of the house," Albert says. His plan incorporates high-quality materials along with meticulous placement of fixtures to make the most of the space.

BORROWED SPACES. A bump-out extending into the laundry area provides enough space for a private toilet compartment but saves the couple the expense of having to move the laundry room. A new stacked washer and dryer prevents the reworked laundry area from feeling too small.

TWO PERSON SHOWER. A wall-mounted walnut vanity seemingly floats above the floor. Low-voltage toe-kick lighting enhances the illusion. A two-person shower replaces the tub and includes a seating bench with two shower arms and four showerheads. A sandblasted window within the shower area lets in light without sacrificing privacy.

WARM FLOORS. Limestone tiles cover the floor, vanity counter, shower floor, and mirror surround. Copper accent tiles set into the limestone add color and texture. Radiant heating coils installed beneath the stone make the floors feel warm and toasty.

SOPHISTICATED DECOR. Colors are soft and neutral, creating a soothing and inviting ambience. Glass blocks cover the shower walls. The remaining drywall is covered in torn wallpaper in an earth-tone print. The wallpaper is applied like a collage to resemble natural stone. A brushed or satin finish on the faucets and fixtures enhances the minimalist look of the room.

"The key to good design is incorporating as many of the owners' wishes into the project with respect to the architecture and with regard to their budget."

ALBERT CAREY

"Everyone had very different designs, but there was one I knew that was right for us the moment I saw it," homeowner Kim Chung says. "Michelle and Camille's plan really used the available space, and the design was very inviting."

WHAT MAKES THIS PLAN WORK? The compartmentalized plan *opposite* and *below left* enables the bath to serve multiple purposes: as a guest bath, as a two-person bath when both Kim and Fred need to get ready for work or bed at the same time, and as a tranquil retreat at the end of a long day. Unique details abound in this bath, including the shallow sink *right* and *below right*.

HOW CAN YOU GET THE LOOK? To create a tranquil *feng shui* retreat of your own, read books or visit some of the myriad online resources. Even if you don't choose to follow all *feng shui* principles, consider some of the general guidelines to add function to your bath. Creating specialized compartments, for example, enables you to comfortably share the space with someone else.

DID THE DESIGNERS MEET THE BUDGET? The Chungs increased their budget significantly so that they could upgrade the new laundry center simultaneously. The laundry center features a water-saving washer and dryer, and custom cabinetry complete with storage cubbies and a folding counter. Additional features added as the remodeling progressed include a faucet that fills the tub from the ceiling and radiant-heat floors. The Chungs changed contractors halfway through the project, further increasing the overall costs. For more information about choosing professionals, see *page 184*. **ACTUAL COST** $120,000

"Looking at this bath is like looking at a piece of artwork in and of itself," Kim Chung says. "The fire wall is the ultimate focal point in the room."

AHHH SPA

Spa baths like the Chungs' retreat exude serenity with neutral colors and smooth finishes. Consider the following as you plan your spalike bath getaway.

● OUTDOOR CONNECTION. Natural textures, such as warm wood finishes, and earthy elements, such as natural stone floors or counters and live plants, help bring the outdoors in. Natural light and fresh air via windows, skylights, or—better yet—glass doors that open to a private garden also freshen the body and spirit.

● PAMPERED BODY, PAMPERED MIND. Luxury amenities, such as heated floors and heated towel bars, can make entering and exiting the bath and shower welcome events.

● LUXURIOUS ACCESSORIES. To make your bath experience even more enjoyable, stock up on indulgent accessories, such as thick Egyptian cotton towels, heavy terry-cloth robes, soothing soaps and bath oils, and scented candles.

BEFORE THE MAKEOVER

SOMETHING EXTRA. A few feet of space was gained in the front portion of the bathroom when the demolition team discovered that plumbing lines were taking up less space than originally thought. The added square footage allows room for a built-in bench with storage cubbies underneath *opposite.* The candlelit wall *above left* illustrates the *feng shui* principle of fire. The new laundry room *above* fills space once occupied by a closet below the stairs.

1 ROOM 3 WAYS

designers' challenge

old-world accents

BEFORE THE MAKEOVER

Rick Blanchard and Lisa Jackson asked three designers to develop a plan that gives their dysfunctional kitchen saucy Spanish flare—within a budget of $50,000.

DESIGNER BARRY KORN CKD, NKBA, CREATIVE KITCHEN DESIGN

TWO ROOMS IN ONE. To make the kitchen feel larger and work harder, Barry recommends removing the wall between the existing laundry room and kitchen. The washer and dryer remain in their current locations but are now hidden behind bifold doors. A large pantry cabinet and broom closet are added to the old laundry space, and the refrigerator is relocated nearer to this new storage to create a convenient spot for unloading groceries.

ARCHED ENTRANCE. To promote the breakfast room as a focal point of the design—and to make it feel more connected to the redesigned kitchen—the peninsula that separates it from the work core is removed, and a new Spanish-feel archway is added. "We want to keep the breakfast room and its unique ceiling contour as it is," Barry explains. The peninsula cooktop and nearby wall ovens are removed, and a new range and custom hood are added to the wall opposite the sink.

RAISED-PANEL CABINETRY. Three cabinetry options feature raised-panel doors. Any of the options can be stained in one of three warm wood tones to visually contrast with the stained wood floor.

TOUCHABLE SURFACES. Sparkling Uba Tuba granite is planned for the countertops. Alternating wide and narrow-width wood planks, used on the existing floor in the living room, continue in the breakfast room and kitchen to create a seamless look.

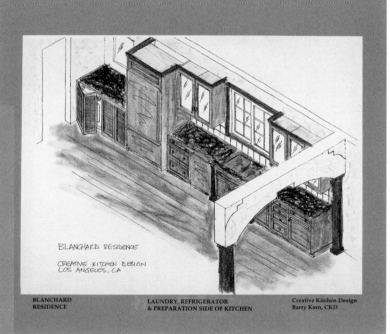
BLANCHARD RESIDENCE

CREATIVE KITCHEN DESIGN
LOS ANGELES, CA

BLANCHARD
RESIDENCE

LAUNDRY, REFRIGERATOR
& PREPARATION SIDE OF KITCHEN

Creative Kitchen Design
Barry Korn, CKD

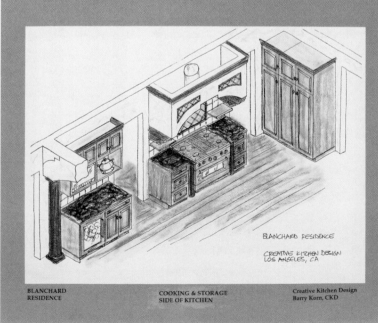
BLANCHARD RESIDENCE

CREATIVE KITCHEN DESIGN
LOS ANGELES, CA

BLANCHARD
RESIDENCE

COOKING & STORAGE
SIDE OF KITCHEN

Creative Kitchen Design
Barry Korn, CKD

"My passion is to make a kitchen function as beautifully as it looks. Today's kitchens are similar to what log cabins were 100 years ago: Families use the kitchen for nearly every daily activity." BARRY KORN

DESIGNER RON WOODSON, RON WOODSON FINE ART AND DESIGN

OPEN PLAN. Ron's plan features a user-friendly layout and a breakfast room filled with Spanish charm. Similar to Barry Korn's arrangement (see *page 119*), the peninsula between the breakfast room and kitchen is removed, and the kitchen work core expands into the laundry room to increase storage possibilities.

VIBRANT COLORS. A new farm-style apron sink—red with bronze faucets—becomes a focal point in the newly designed space. The sink is surrounded by warm maple cabinets, rich walnut floors, and ruby-red granite countertops. A red tile backsplash enlivens the walls; a Spanish-inspired mosaic brings exciting color to the wall behind the range.

ELEGANT BREAKFAST ROOM. Completely open to the kitchen, the breakfast area features deep red velvet draperies and an octagon-shape area rug. A period chandelier, which complements the other design elements in the kitchen, illuminates the breakfast table.

"My personal design aesthetic is a clean and simple layout with an ambience of warmth and serenity." RON WOODSON

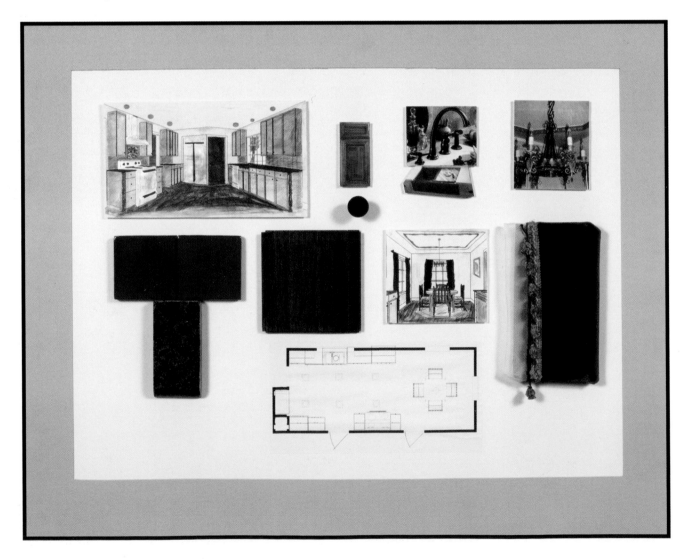

3

DESIGNER DOLORES ESPARZA, DOLORES ESPARZA INTERIOR AND ARCHITECTURAL DESIGNS

OLD-WORLD ACCENTS. Dolores's plan combines rustic Spanish details with colorful focal points, including a stained-glass window above the kitchen sink and a gourmet cooking center on the opposite side of the room.

SEPARATE LAUNDRY. The peninsula is removed to ease traffic congestion. The laundry area remains intact, but the doorway and a section of the wall are removed, making both rooms feel larger. A new arched niche adorns the remaining portion of the laundry room wall and provides attractive display space.

GLASS DOORS. To bring more light into the room, a pair of French doors is added to the sink wall.

ORIGINAL DETAILING. Custom cabinetry throughout the remodeled space mimics the architectural detailing found on the existing front door of the home, tying the new kitchen to the original architecture. A multistep painted and glazed finish gives the cabinetry a timeworn look. A colorful tile backsplash combines with a ceramic mosaic behind the range, while a muted camel-color travertine tile floor with a centuries-old appearance completes the old-world theme.

"I try to bring my designs back to the original architecture of the home, so that when you walk in the door you feel like you are stepping back in time."

DOLORES ESPARZA

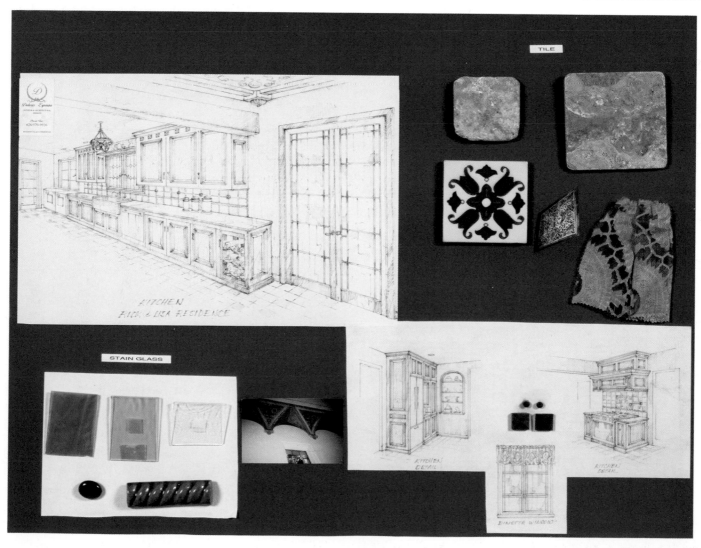

3

Designer Dolores Esparza gave the owners the old-world look and the layout they were hoping for. "The Spanish-theme kitchen appears authentic to the house, which is exactly what we wanted," homeowner Lisa Jackson says.

WHAT MAKES THIS PLAN WORK? Rearranging the appliances *opposite* saves steps when preparing meals and enables Rick and Lisa to cook together without getting in one another's way. Utilizing a partial wall between the kitchen and laundry area keeps both spaces intact—so that the counter and work space can be shared between the two work areas whenever necessary. New French doors open the entire area to natural light and views, and the new courtyard beyond the doors allows the couple to cook and entertain both inside and out with ease.

HOW CAN YOU GET THE LOOK? Attention to detail and the skilled handiwork of various artisans made a timeworn look come alive for these homeowners. To give your kitchen similar rustic flavor, distress your cabinets with sandpaper, paint, and glaze. Cover floors and backsplashes with honed-stone tiles that have an authentic aged look and dot the countertops with collectibles gathered from flea markets and import stores.

DID THE DESIGNER MEET THE BUDGET? Rick and Lisa increased their original $50,000 budget to include professional-grade appliances *opposite* and higher-price fixtures *below.* "The plasterlike wall finish was also a last-minute decision that caused a budget increase," Rick explains. **ACTUAL COST** $65,000

BEFORE THE MAKEOVER

VINTAGE OR REPRODUCTION?

If you're courting visions of an all-vintage room, whether it's old world or 1950s kitsch, be prepared to visit antiques shops and salvage yards with a keen eye or substitute reproductions for authentic fixtures and fittings. A reproduction faucet (shown *above right*) often can have the same aesthetics as vintage fixtures, and many feature lifetime warranties on parts and finishes. Reporcelainized sinks, although durable, will not last as long as quality new models, like the one *above right,* that have been designed to look old. Chandeliers and vintage light fixtures can be rewired to meet today's safety standards, but make sure you purchase these antiques from a reputable dealer. Before installing any vintage fixture, have a master plumber or electrician inspect the item to ensure it meets current manufacturing codes.

VINTAGE CHARM. Distressed cabinets and a custom-made hood *above left* look as though they've always been a part of the Mediterranean-style home. New stained-glass windows over the sink *above* feature the same colors as the tile mural above the range, bringing continuity to the separate work spaces. New amenities include the compact wine refrigerator and double French patio doors *left.* With an antique chandelier overhead, a new iron-clad table and chairs makes the adjoining breakfast area *opposite* as inviting as the formal dining room beyond.

"The other designs didn't have as much of an old-world feel; they would have looked like remodeled kitchens," homeowner Rick Blanchard says. "When you step into this space, you step back in time."

1ROOM
3WAYS

designers'challenge

hotelsuiteretreat

Nancy and Jim Cole asked designers to rework their long-neglected master bedroom into a relaxing in-home haven with a budget of $25,000.

BEFORE THE MAKEOVER

DESIGNER KAREN BEGAN IDS, IND,
KB DESIGNS

INCREASED VOLUME. "My vision for Nancy and Jim Cole's project is to create a suite that has an understated elegance," Karen says. Raising the ceiling from 8 to 11 feet to create a coffered-style ceiling increases the volume of the room, making it appear grander.

HARDWOOD FLOORS. A wood plank floor in a dark umber color replaces worn carpet. Creamy caramel-color walls complement the dark floor and make the room feel cozy. A paler shade of caramel on the ceiling visually pushes the ceiling even higher above the new floor. The existing flat-panel doors are replaced with more traditional six-panel wooden doors that are finished in white or cream to complement the woodwork. Plantation shutters are repaired and repainted to look like new—at a fourth of the cost of replacements.

ISLAND-INSPIRED BED. The bed moves to the wall below the existing shuttered windows to create a dramatic focal point. A soft chenille duvet cover in a sage-green hue tucks beneath the mattress. Fabrics with island-inspired prints adorn the bed pillows and dust ruffle. A new upholstered settee at the foot of the bed and a variety of throw pillows are covered in a bright contrasting print fabric. By the existing side window, a cushioned wooden lounging chair and a round mahogany side table provide a spot for reading and relaxing.

CUSTOM CABINET. A custom-built entertainment center features numerous storage drawers and two frosted-glass storage cabinets that conceal audiovisual equipment. A flat-screen plasma television slides into a central cubby.

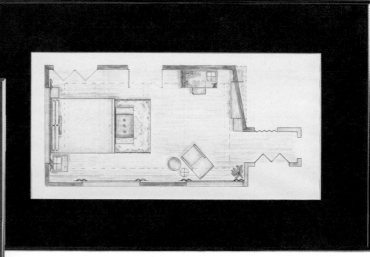

"My passion for design is getting things done quickly and on time and ensuring that all the follow-through is complete."   KAREN BEGAN

DESIGNER JONE PENCE ASID, CID, JONE PENCE INTERIOR DESIGN & CONSTRUCTION

2

OUTDOOR CONNECTION. "The Coles' suite needs to be comfortable and relaxed while bringing the outdoors in," Jone says. Rearranging the furniture provides enough exterior wall space for a sliding French door that will open to a private patio garden. Adjacent to the patio door, a small sitting area provides a spot for the couple to relax and read.

WALL OF ART. "The hall entrance to the suite is moved to create a more dramatic view of the suite when you first walk into the room," Jone explains. "By moving the door down, I am also able to create a wonderful art wall." The suite features artwork with floral motifs in vivid colors.

CHEERFUL COLORS. Walls throughout the suite are painted a warm yellow, and new off-white crown molding adds architectural interest to the ceiling line. Updated carpet features a textured weave that feels warm and soft underfoot. A new custom-made mahogany bed is accentuated with white-on-white patterned linens and deep red accent pillows. Tropical-print draperies replace existing shutters and make the room feel richer and cozier.

CLOSET MAKEOVERS. Reapportioning the space in the largest of the two existing closets increases storage. The smaller closet is opened up to create built-in drawers and shelves; an office niche across from the bed houses the TV, computer, and audiovisual equipment.

TASK LIGHTING. Recessed lights installed in the sitting area and on each side of the bed shine down for reading and are switched separately so that both Nancy and Jim can operate them from under the covers.

"Attention to detail is really important when choosing the fabrics, finishes, colors, architectural details, and especially the lighting. Each element enhances the comfort and ease of the finished design."

JONE PENCE

Jone Pence, A.S.I.D., C.I.D.
Interior Design & Construction

Fabrics

Furniture Floor Plan

Furniture & Wood Finishes

Bed Finish

Carpet

Pillows

Paint Colors

Walls   Trim

3

DESIGNERS LINDA EVARTS ALLIED ASID, & JEREMY EVARTS, MARK'S CARPET AND DESIGN

ECLECTIC FURNISHINGS. Linda and Jeremy's plan proposes custom-designed furnishings inspired by Asian antiques. "The vision that we share for the Cole project is that the room be comfortable and functional, but also charming and sophisticated," Jeremy says.

VAULTED CEILING. Raising the ceiling to expose the structural beams increases the volume of the room, making it feel even larger. Camel-color paint warms the walls, and a lighter neutral tone accentuates the ceiling beams. New pale honey-color carpeting warms the floor. Pull-down shades softened by a silk banner-top treatment replace existing shutters.

CUSTOM STORAGE. The small closet is eliminated, and a clothes hutch and bookcases are added. Custom cabinets with bamboo accents hold the computer and the television. The large closet wall is moved down to make the interior large enough to house both Nancy and Jim's clothing.

COZY FIREPLACE. The new closet wall is angled at the corner to allow room for a new gas or electric fireplace. Across from the fireplace, two cozy reading chairs and a small table are illuminated by beaded hanging lanterns. A custom-made antique-reproduction wooden bed and a matching nightstand create a second decorative focal point.

"I prefer to use a little bit of eclecticism in my design, creating the illusion that a project was completed over a long period. That way the finished result never looks dated." LINDA EVARTS

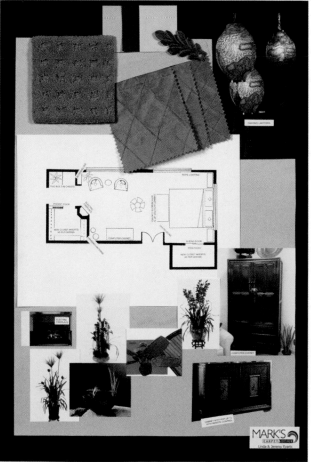

2 "We liked the way Jone reworked the layout so we could add glass doors and a new private patio," homeowner Nancy Cole says.

WHAT MAKES THIS PLAN WORK? Furniture, doorways, and closets are reworked, opening up enough floor space for an office niche, complete with a computer and a TV that can be viewed from the bed. Adjacent to the niche and in front of the new sliding door, a small sitting area *left* enables the couple to relax and unwind at the end of a busy day. A new armoire across from the closet door contains off-season clothing, freeing storage space in the closet.

HOW CAN YOU GET THE LOOK? The Coles wanted their master suite to look like a vacation getaway *below*, so they chose colors and fabrics reminiscent of rooms they visited during their travels. To give your bedroom a luxury hotel look, gather brochures from favorite resorts and search the Internet for a resort room with amenities you'd like to have at home. Then choose paints, fabrics, and furnishings that emulate the ambience.

DID THE DESIGNER MEET THE BUDGET? The budget provided enough for the straightforward structural changes as well as all the furnishings and accessories. After the remodeling, the couple invested in a new TV for the office niche. **ACTUAL COST** $25,000

"Dimmer switches tucked behind the curtains by the bed control lighting throughout the room," designer *Jone Pence explains.*

BEFORE THE MAKEOVER

"Adding the private patio extended our bedroom to the outdoors," Nancy Cole says. "We love reading and listening to the water fountain in the new garden."

HOW MUCH SHOULD YOU SPEND?

To determine an appropriate budget for your makeover, seek bids from three or more reputable designers. (For help finding designers, see *page 184*.) If their estimates are out of line with your vision, ask for suggestions on how to scale back. If the plans are still bigger than your wallet, try these tips to help you save.

● CHOOSE MORE-AFFORDABLE MATERIALS. Birch cabinets cost up to three times less than solid cherry and can be customized with stains or paint. Combine stock with semicustom cabinets to save additional funds. Laminate floors are less costly to install than solid wood planks, granite tiles less than slabs. (For more information on materials, see *pages 170–183*.)

● GET FREE HELP. Swap jobs with handy neighbors—you can paint their interiors while they tackle your wiring.

● ASSIST AS A GENERAL LABORER. Consider wallpapering, painting, and doing the cleanup yourself. A cost-plus-fixed-fee contract will credit your labor against a contractor's fee.

● COMPARE PRICES. Your designer may get a discount on many products, but you may pay even less if you shop for your own materials.

● PLAN AROUND FEATURES. Keep costly-to-move elements, such as chimneys, in their current locations. Leave exterior openings where they are and cut back on any costly structural changes, such as raising a ceiling.

AT-HOME RETREAT. Classically styled furnishings *opposite* combine with creamy white and butterscotch tone-on-tone fabrics—accented with dollops of deep red—to create a sophisticated ambience similar to that found in a five-star hotel. A built-in office area *above*, complete with a flat-panel television, offers ample storage and display space for working at home.

BEFORE THE MAKEOVER

1 ROOM 3 WAYS

designers'challenge **continuity with comfort**

Kim and John Shohfi asked designers to transform their galley into an efficient and attractive kitchen perfect for cooking and entertaining on a budget of $80,000.

BEFORE THE MAKEOVER

DESIGNERS JANET BUSSELL & BARRIE LIVINGSTONE, ASID, BUSSELL LIVINGSTONE INTERIORS, INC.

TWICE THE SIZE. In Janet and Barrie's design, old-world charm mixes with cutting-edge materials. The wall that formerly housed the cooktop is removed, doubling the size of the work core. A new pantry cabinet, designed to look like a freestanding armoire, offers ample storage for dry goods and serving pieces. A new built-in desk provides a spot for organizing paperwork and recipes. An 8-foot-long center island houses a second sink and provides enough work space for a second cook.

UNITED FRONT. Dark-stained hardwood floors replace terra-cotta tiles, and custom-glazed raised-panel cabinets meld the kitchen with the rest of the traditional home. White woodwork is painted to match the color of the new floors. A heavily veined marble slab tops the island, and complementary sand-tone French limestone covers the perimeter counters. Vintage reproduction Malibu tiles bring welcome texture and dots of color to the backsplash.

RECYCLED APPLIANCES. Because Kim and John's current stainless-steel appliances are nearly new and in good shape, they are used in the redesigned space.

AMPLE LIGHTING. Recessed lights combine with a hanging fixture to increase both ambient and task lighting. Bamboo blinds or Roman shades provide simple yet elegant window treatments that complement the existing farm-style table and chairs.

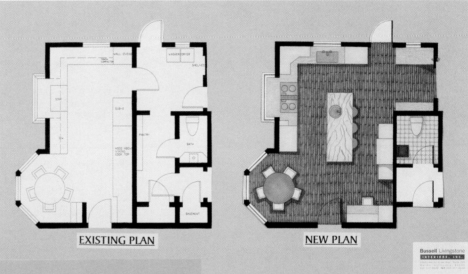

EXISTING PLAN

NEW PLAN

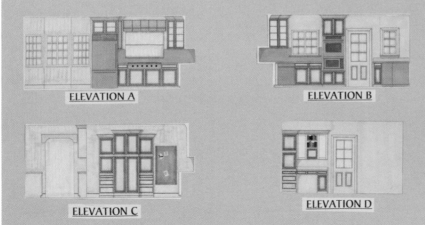

ELEVATION A

ELEVATION B

ELEVATION C

ELEVATION D

"The philosophy and aesthetic that we apply to our projects is that we remain true to the architectural style of the house while bringing in the modern, functional elements our clients desire."

BARRIE LIVINGSTONE

2

DESIGNER PAMELA MUNSON ASID, CBD, MUNSON AND COMPANY, INC.

BACKYARD VIEWS. In Pamela's design English Tudor accents mix with a functional center-island plan. A powder room is moved to the opposite wall of the kitchen so that the kitchen can be oriented toward the backyard and the views. The opening between the kitchen and family room is enlarged to make the rooms feel more connected. The old breakfast area becomes a larger breakfast room that is open to the new kitchen work core.

TWO-TONE CABINETS. A custom-made maple work island, modeled after a hand-carved antique, is stained a deep coffee color.

The cabinets are painted a creamy white and are glazed with a coffee-color stain; the cabinets provide visual contrast against the wood-tone center island.

NATURE-INSPIRED SURFACES. Taupe and cream Mojave granite countertops complement both shades of the new cabinetry; three-dimensional tiles adorned with a pinecone motif protect the backsplash. A wide wood-plank floor is scraped and sanded to create the appearance of natural aging. At the owners' request, all existing appliances, with the exception of the wall ovens, are used in the new layout.

IMPORTED FABRICS. Imported European fabrics used on the island stools and for the window valances reflect the English character of the home.

> *"I look for the best features in the home and then match the client's needs to that style."*
>
> PAMELA MUNSON

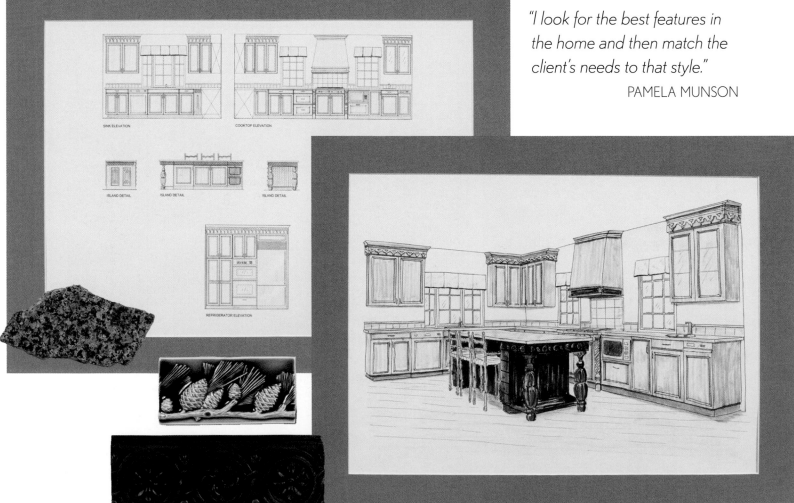

3

DESIGNERS AMNON DAHAN & SHACHAR RONEN, THE XLART GROUP, INC.

SPANISH ACCENTS. Designers Amnon and Shachar envision a sophisticated chef's kitchen with a mix of Spanish and Tudor touches.

OPEN PLAN. Interior walls separating the kitchen from a pantry closet and half bath are removed, opening up the space. A larger arched opening between the family room and the kitchen connects the two rooms and mimics the archways present elsewhere in the home.

FOCAL-POINT ISLAND. The freestanding kitchen island the couple requested is a focal point; it is topped with a dual surface of hardworking butcher block and dramatic blue Brazilian granite. The perimeter counters are topped with a more subdued stone to keep the focus on the island; tumbled marble protects the backsplash. The existing stainless-steel appliances, with the exception of the wall ovens, are used in the new plan.

OPTIMAL STORAGE. Cream-color traditional-style cabinets intersperse with glass-front display cases to double the existing storage capacity. Opposite the new island, a large pantry cabinet replaces the existing pantry closet.

PERIOD DETAILS. Nonstructural exposed beams are added to the ceiling to complement the styling of the makeover. Elegant crown molding and hardwood flooring, stained in a hickory color, complete the room.

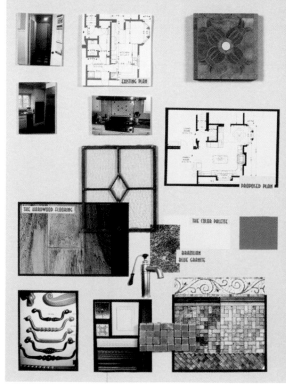

"We make sure to keep a good energy flow between the design and the family that lives in the house." AMNON DAHAN

"It was extremely difficult to choose between the three plans because each one offered an excellent solution to the galley's challenges," homeowner John Shohfi explains. The decision came down to personality: "Barrie and Janet's personalities really clicked with ours, and we thought that would make the whole process a lot of fun," Kim Shohfi says.

WHAT MAKES THIS PLAN WORK? A new L-shape work core combines with a long center island *opposite* to provide an efficient plan that offers ample work surfaces for multiple cooks. In a departure from Barrie and Janet's original plan, the island runs perpendicular to the range and parallel to the sink, maximizing floor space and allowing room for a beverage center and a larger opening to the family room. A second sink in the island takes the pressure off the main sink and is convenient to the snack bar. A below-the-counter microwave, also fitted into the island, enables the Shohfis' young children to use the appliance at will.

HOW CAN YOU GET THE LOOK? To make your kitchen look as though it was furnished over time—as were most early 20th-century kitchens—combine painted and stained cabinets as shown *opposite*. Match design details, such as moldings and corbels, to the original architecture of your home; then coat fresh drywall with a heavily textured and painted finish that resembles old plaster as shown *left*.

DID THE DESIGNERS MEET THE BUDGET? The Shohfis increased their budget by $40,000 so that they could get everything they desired, including new windows, new plumbing and electrical, and a fully stocked beverage center. "The original design we presented matched the budget, but as the planning process continued, the couple's vision for the space grew along with the possibilities," Barrie explains. "The final outcome is everything they wanted and more."

ACTUAL COST $120,000

BEFORE THE MAKEOVER

BEFORE THE MAKEOVER

"A good designer listens to the homeowners and comes up with a plan that is practical and beautiful while matching needs to budget," designer Barrie Livingstone explains.

THE KITCHEN ZONE

The traditional approach to kitchen design has long held the work triangle—an imaginary line connecting the range, refrigerator, and primary sink—to be the basis of the most efficient kitchens. That's because food preparation, cooking, and cleanup typically involve choreographing movement among these three elements. Today's designs step beyond the triangle to include additional work areas, or zones, that comfortably accommodate the activities that occur most often in kitchens. Typically these work areas revolve around a central island, especially one equipped with a second sink as shown *right* or a cooktop. Specialty storage features, such as the pullout spice rack *above left*, make these zones more efficient. For kitchens designed to accommodate two or more cooks, as in the Shohfis' kitchen, an island can also serve as a shared point in creating two or more work areas. When planning the layout of your kitchen, consider adding workstations to serve your special needs and interests, such as multiple cooks, buffet service *above right*, child's play, or baking.

"A part of what makes a new space look like it has always been in the home is giving it authenticity," designer Barrie Livingstone explains. To accomplish this, the design team matched colors and surfaces to those used during the era the home was built.

PIECES OF THE PAST. Opening up the ceiling above the eating area *right* offered a pleasant surprise—exposed beams that complement the architecture of the Tudor home. Adorned with a hand-painted floral motif, the new plastered range hood *above* looks as though it has always been a part of the home. Vintage reproduction backsplashes tiles *above right* look equally antiquated. Painting and distressing the once-pristine white window trim in the breakfast room *opposite* instantly ages it and connects the new space to its Tudor roots.

BEFORE THE MAKEOVER

1ROOM
3WAYS

designers'challenge

picture **perfect**

With a budget of $35,000, Jerry and Nettie Wolak asked design experts to revamp their master bath and closet into functional spaces with old-world flair.

BEFORE THE MAKEOVER

DESIGNER RICHARD W. HERB ALLIED ASID, RICHARD W. HERB INTERIORS

STRUCTURAL CHALLENGE. "The Jerry and Nettie Wolak project is a huge challenge. There are some structural aspects to the house—the way it's configured and the fact that the master bath is on the second floor—that had to be taken into consideration," Richard says.

TRIPLE STORAGE. The new layout turns the square footage taken up by the old master bath into closet space, tripling the amount of storage space. The former sitting area in the bedroom becomes the new master bath as well as an entryway into the master suite from the upstairs hall.

ARTFUL ARCHWAYS. Traditional European-style columns and archways accentuate a whirlpool tub and a glass-tiled shower. Arched mirrors top off double vanities that are separated by a lowered makeup center. The granite tub deck extends into the shower to create a stone seat. Complementary stone tiles cover the floor throughout the master bath.

OIL-RUBBED CABINETRY. Custom cabinets feature flat-panel doors and an oil-rubbed bronze finish. Countertop surface options include stone tiles or granite slabs in either a combination of terra-cottas, earthy browns, and blues, or creamy neutrals and beiges.

ARTIST'S MURAL. The long wall of the entryway features a hand-painted Tuscan-style mural.

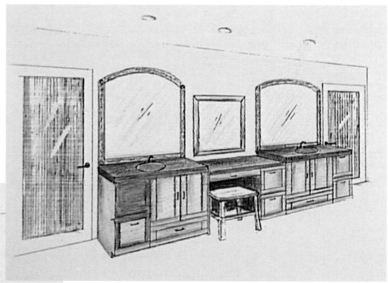

"When working with a couple, you have two different people with two different sets of ideas and yet one project. You need to meld those ideas together to make sure you accomplish the end goal for the couple."

RICHARD W. HERB

DESIGNER MICHELE STONE, MICHELE STONE INTERIOR DESIGN, & CONTRACTOR DAVID REAUME, DAVID REAUME CONSTRUCTION AND DESIGN

DOUBLE-SIDED FIREPLACE. Michele and David's plan uses color, texture, and a fireplace to create a warm and cozy retreat. "Nettie and Jerry's space is very interesting because their bathroom is very small, but they have this underutilized sitting area next to it which is fairly good size," David says. "That gives us the ability to expand the bathroom and give them a much larger closet."

THREE SEPARATE SPACES. By moving existing walls and adding new ones, the team increases the size of the bath and doubles the size of the closet while keeping a smaller sitting room intact. The double-sided fireplace can be viewed from either the spa-style tub or the sitting room opposite. An 8-foot-wide open archway connects the bedroom to the sitting area and offers a view of the fireplace from the bed.

BACKYARD VIEW. A window installed above the new tub offers a view of the backyard and increases the amount of daylight that penetrates the space. A marble platform on the tub deck extends into the shower to create a seat.

MULTIPLE TEXTURES. Custom cabinetry is painted a creamy white and distressed to look centuries old. Stone tiles carved in a rope pattern accentuate the vanity mirror. Crown and baseboard moldings are made from a complementary ceramic. Soft camel-color silk Roman shades cover the window above the tub. Complementary drapery panels adorn the windows in the sitting room.

RELAXED AMBIENCE. "Overall the bath is going to be very soothing and calm, with touches of amber and beige—the perfect place to unwind," Michele says.

"The most important concept to design is to keep the interior design architecturally sound as well as make it inviting and usable." MICHELE STONE

WOLAK
MASTER BATH

3

DESIGNER DAN BISSELL ASID, DAN BISSELL INTERIOR DESIGN

HEXAGONAL ENTRANCE. Dan's plan features an entry vestibule that leads into the master suite: The master bedroom is situated to the right, while the master bath is located on the left.

FUNCTIONAL BATH. The new bath layout features separate built-in vanities with arched soffits, a large whirlpool tub, a separate glass-enclosed shower, and a private toilet compartment. Vanities are made from alder wood and are coated in a dark walnut stain. His-and-hers closets are located on opposite corners of the bath.

CENTERED CHANDELIER. Existing windows are removed and replaced with a new larger window above the tub. A chandelier hung in the center of the room enhances natural light. Earthy brown stone tiles cover the floor and counters.

DRAMATIC DECOR. Decorative three-dimensional accent tiles adorn the backsplash. Faux-plaster painted walls add old-world-style texture and drama. An open-weave scarf valance tops the tub window and disguises privacy shades.

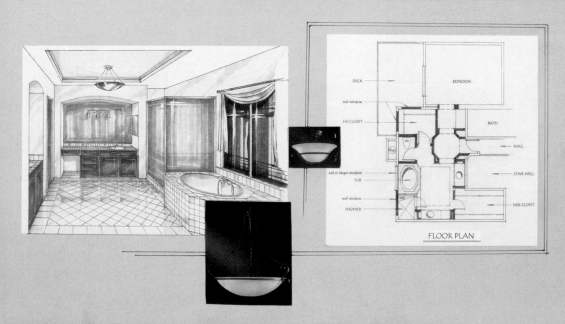

"A room that is accessorized well makes a complete design statement. Accessories are the icing on the cake."

DAN BISSELL

2

"It took us the entire week to make our decision," homeowner Nettie Wolak says. "After lots of contemplation, we chose David and Michele's design. We had the best time working with them because they were such a dynamic team."

WHAT MAKES THIS PLAN WORK? A smaller, more inviting sitting area separates the bedroom from the bath and provides a welcome entrance into the suite from the upstairs hall. A new fireplace *opposite* can be viewed from the bath, the sitting area, and the adjacent bedroom. On the bath side, niches above the fireplace provide space for a television and artwork. The raised stone hearth extends around the corner of the bath to create a seamless tub deck and an adjacent shower seat, separated only by a wall of tempered glass. A privacy wall next to the shower defines a toilet niche. Unused space under the eaves creates an L-shape closet that is twice as large as the original.
HOW CAN YOU GET THE LOOK? Creamy shades of amber and beige *above left* create a tranquil and romantic ambience and visually tie the

BEFORE THE MAKEOVER

three spaces together. To create a similar mood in your bath, choose surfaces in neutral or pastel shades and pay attention to every detail—such as the decorative tiles *above right*. Mellow tones soften the look of the design and encourage rest and relaxation. Introduce a variety of textures, such as tumbled stone floors and shiny granite countertops, then increase the feeling of comfort by adding stacks of luxurious towels and indulgent accessories, such as aromatic bath salts.
DID THE DESIGNERS MEET THE BUDGET? The owners increased their budget by several thousand dollars so that they could accessorize the sitting area and bath with new furniture, artwork, and accessories. A professional closet organizer also customized the new closet to meet Nettie and Jerry's specific storage needs. **ACTUAL COST** $45,000

INSTANT AGE. Instead of choosing a painted cabinetry finish as the design team originally presented, the couple opted for an old-fashioned oiled- and rubbed-wood finish *this photo*. Vintage reproduction bronze hardware *opposite top left* complements the traditional styling of the bath and makes the new space appear timeworn.

"We debated about increasing the budget, but in the end we are glad we did," Nettie Wolak says. "The suite has become our favorite place in the house. We can't even believe it's our house—from the mantel and the beautiful fireplace surround to the custom furnishings and artwork. It's absolutely incredible."

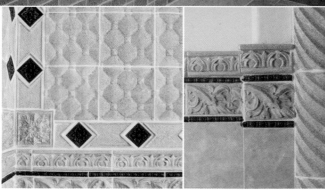

MATCHING FORM TO FUNCTION

An extension of the new bath, the sitting room *above* provides a quiet, romantic retreat for a couple with two young children. When planning your bath, think beyond the basic box. Bathrooms can be open to the sun and the sky, a favorite garden, or a chic coffee bar. Because bathrooms are the most personal room in the house, they are the ideal place to let your personality shine. The Wolaks' appreciation for traditional styling and artistry is conveyed through their selection of tiles and columns *left* and *above left*. The roomy shower *opposite* encourages relaxation. When creating baths designed for specific family members, plan the space with the look and feel that appeals to those people, not what a few visitors might expect to see.

1 ROOM 3 WAYS

designers' challenge a cook's kitchen

The Penmans asked designers to create a gourmet kitchen—with a budget of $65,000.

BEFORE THE MAKEOVER

DESIGNERS CYNTHIA PIANA ASID, IDS, NKBA, & LORI SOUZA WHFA, PIANA INTERIORS, INC.

GRAND PLAN. "When we found out Ray and Pamela Penman went to Paris for their honeymoon, we were inspired to create a chef's kitchen with a classic European look," Cynthia says. A dual-island layout provides room for multiple cooks and guests.

FOCUS ON ENTERTAINING. The existing bar wall between the kitchen and family room is removed to make casual entertaining more comfortable and convenient. The island closest to the family room acts as a bar and is equipped with a wine refrigerator and comfy barstools.

FAUX STONE. Faux French limestone countertops look like real stone but are more durable and resistant to stains. The existing wood floor is extended into the adjacent family room, visually connecting the two spaces.

INSTANT AGE. The ceiling is updated with salvaged wood beams that look as though they've always been a part of the home. The cabinets are painted, then rubbed and distressed to create a timeworn appearance. Vintage-look, handmade ceramic tiles are accented with three-dimensional fruit motifs, bringing dollops of color into the room.

FUNCTIONAL LIGHT. Downlights combine with undercounter lighting to illuminate each work surface. A vintage-look chandelier adds drama above the central island.

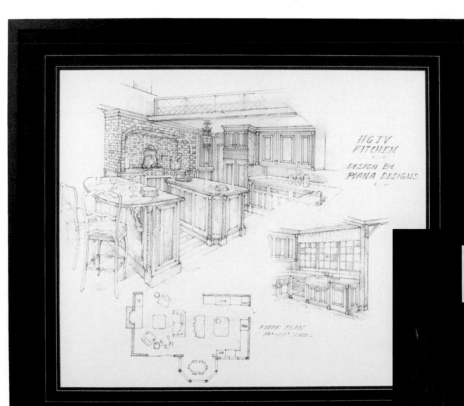

"To effectively communicate with clients, you need to be able to tune into what they're not saying, take a good look at the things they're pulling from magazines, and incorporate that into their everyday lifestyle." LORI SOUZA

DESIGNER JANE BROOKS ASID, JANE BROOKS INTERIORS

ITALIAN GRACE, AMERICAN FUNCTION. Jane envisions an elegant Tuscan kitchen in a jewel-tone palette. She replaces the wet bar between the kitchen and family room with an L-shape peninsula. Wooden cabinets throughout the room are stained a light earthy brown. Multitone slate covers the floor, and speckled brown granite tops the counters. Faucets and sinks are made from hammered copper. A prep sink in the peninsula offers cleaning flexibility and enables the homeowners to cook together comfortably. Translucent faux-plaster walls in a creamy beige look centuries old. Professional-grade stainless-steel appliances increase cooking functionality and complement the old-world style.

"My job is to help clients wade through all the design possibilities and make choices that they will appreciate for years to come." JANE BROOKS

IRON WORKS. A Tuscan-style wrought-iron pot rack supplements kitchen storage and shows off beautiful cookware. A matching wrought-iron table and chairs update the breakfast nook. Window treatments and upholstery fabrics in rich colors add warmth to the space.

PICTURE-PERFECT LIGHTING. Pendant lights illuminate the peninsula; accent lighting is installed above the wall cabinets. An elaborate Italian chandelier is a dramatic focal point in the breakfast nook.

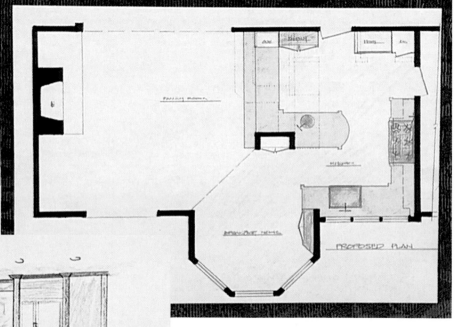

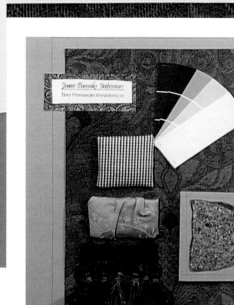

3 DESIGNER ILENE S. CROUPPEN ASID, CID, GEOMETRIX

PRETTY AND PRACTICAL. Ilene envisions a light, open, and thoroughly modern kitchen. The existing bar wall between the kitchen and the family room is removed to allow guests to easily migrate between the two spaces. Top-of-the-line appliances replace existing models, but to eliminate the need for costly rewiring and moving plumbing lines, the new appliances stand in the same places as their predecessors. Molded wood paneling, which is painted white, makes the standard-height ceiling a visual asset. A large double island in a medium wood-tone finish looks like a freestanding antique and provides work space for a second cook. A custom hood above the new range creates a stunning focal point.

TEXTURAL TENACITY. White brick-shape ceramic tiles cover the backsplash; they are enhanced with white three-dimensional decorative tiles. Custom cabinets are painted white and feature raised-panel doors that complement the cabinetry in adjacent rooms. Glass-front cabinets and open shelves combine storage with display. Sand-color stone countertops withstand heat and resist stains. Stained and polished wood planks warm the floor.

MOOD LIGHTING. To illuminate the space, Ilene suggests directional light for all the work surfaces, enhanced by additional recessed ceiling lights and undercabinet lights. All lights are attached to dimmers so that the couple can change the mood of the room at the turn of a knob.

STORAGE BONANZA. Opposite the sink a wall of cabinets is entirely dedicated to storage. New bookshelves wrap around the windows in the breakfast nook to hold Pamela's extensive cookbook collection.

FAMILY CONNECTION. The fireplace in the adjacent family room is updated with new tiles and a hearth that complement the new surfaces in the kitchen.

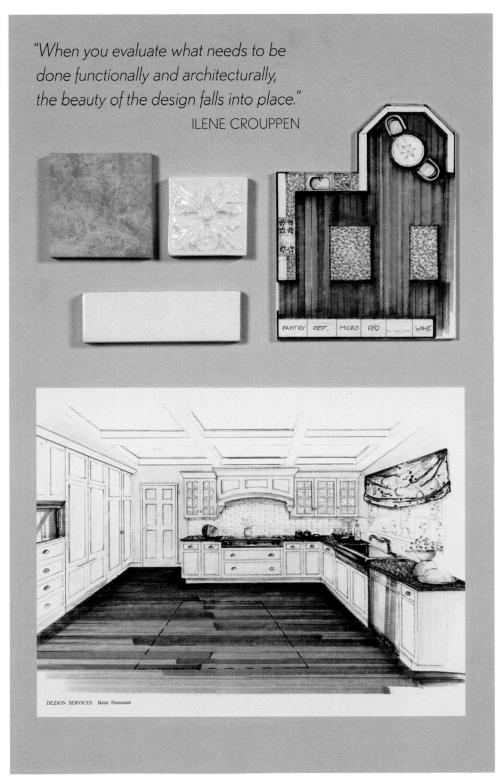

"When you evaluate what needs to be done functionally and architecturally, the beauty of the design falls into place."
ILENE CROUPPEN

PANTRY REF. MICRO D/O ___ WINE

DEZIGN SERVICES Bette Hornstien

3 "All the plans were gorgeous, but Ilene's design was the most livable and the most complementary to the existing architecture in our home," homeowner Pamela Penman says.

WHAT MAKES THIS PLAN WORK? The double-island layout *left* keeps traffic flowing smoothly and provides room for cooks and guests to mingle in the space. Functional amenities abound and include a pot-filler faucet by the stove, a warming drawer and microwave built into the storage wall, and a wine refrigerator.

HOW CAN YOU GET THE LOOK? "The secret to creating a gorgeous all-white kitchen is to add as much texture as possible," Ilene says. In the Penmans' kitchen, textural variation is seen in the backsplash, the countertops, the flooring, and in the cabinet doors. Use glass-front cabinets and open shelves to highlight additional shapes and shadows, then add warmth and coziness with natural surfaces, such as stone countertops or hardwood floors. For visual variety, change accessories and artwork seasonally.

DID THE DESIGNER MEET THE BUDGET? The Penmans had to significantly increase their budget to remove a load-bearing wall—an unforeseen difficulty—and install a wide structural ceiling beam. Though the project took more than six months to complete and cost more than expected, both homeowners believe the end result was worth the effort.

ACTUAL COST $95,000

BEFORE THE MAKEOVER

BEFORE THE MAKEOVER

"The molded ceiling treatment was one of the reasons we chose Ilene's plan," homeowner Ray Penman says. "It transforms a standard ceiling into an architectural asset."

PROFESSIONAL APPEAL. "The professional appliances enable me to create the recipes and flavors Ray and I love," Pamela says. The range *opposite* with a pot-filler faucet above are two of the couple's favorite features. The vintage-look brick-pattern ceramic tiles that adorn the backsplash *top left* give the new kitchen an old-fashioned appearance.

Across from the sink, the storage wall *left* houses two pantry closets equipped with pullout shelves, the refrigerator, a microwave, and a warming drawer. The area to the left of the microwave doubles as a butler's pantry and houses a wine refrigerator. The shelves *above* were designed to hold Pamela's complete cookbook collection, but the couple opted to display only a few of her favorite books along with some cherished collectibles to prevent a cluttered look.

AWAY WITH WALLS

Tearing down interior walls is almost always less expensive than building an addition, but there are exceptions—as the Penmans discovered—so you should always have a professional review your plans and evaluate your home before you start any demolition project.

Non-load-bearing walls are the least costly to remove because no additional support beams are required. To determine if your wall is load-bearing, look in the basement and upstairs (if applicable). If there isn't a wall above and below the one you are planning to move, it's probably not load-bearing. Seek out plumbing and electrical lines in the basement as well. You'll be able to see where

the lines lead and then you can make a good estimate as to where you'll find them on the main floor.

Removing a load-bearing wall requires the addition of a support beam and is more difficult and costly to do. These projects require professional expertise and can double or even triple the cost of wall removal.

Note that in nearly all remodeling projects there are surprises to overcome, such as a boarded-up chimney, a peculiar bend in a water pipe, or a load-bearing wall that even the professionals didn't catch. Be flexible with your plans and, if possible, keep a contingency budget of at least 10 percent of the total cost so that you can cover such unexpected occurrences.

GREAT ROOM, GREAT STYLE. To make the kitchen and existing family room look like they have always been part of the same great-room, Ilene covered the fireplace hearth and surround *this photo* and *opposite above right* with stone tiles that match the kitchen countertops. New slipcovers update the breakfast room chairs *opposite above left*, and a new area rug *opposite below* warms the new wood floor in the family area.

1 ROOM 3 WAYS

designers'challenge

retreattoluxury

Ed and Margaret Tom challenged designers to develop a plan to fit resort-quality amenities into their small master bath on a budget of $40,000.

BEFORE THE MAKEOVER

DESIGNER MINH-LIEN COHEN ASID, CDESIGN, INC.

PROVIDE PRIVACY. Minh-Lien's design has all the elements of a contemporary spa. "The entrance from the hallway is closed so that access to the bath only comes from the master bedroom, which gives the Toms more privacy," she explains. By closing off another doorway that connects to the dressing area and by removing two interior walls, there is room for a double-sink vanity, a whirlpool tub, and a steam shower. To reduce plumbing costs, the new fixtures hook to existing lines.

LIGHT FLOW. The plan also calls for moving and enlarging the window near the tub, installing recessed lighting throughout the bath, and adding decorative wall sconces on both sides of the mirrors to take advantage of and enhance natural light.

TWICE THE STORAGE. Larger his-and-hers closets fill the existing dressing area that leads to the bathroom. Custom storage racks maximize hanging and shelf space. In the bath proper a small étagère combines with his-and-hers medicine cabinets and the double vanity base to provide ample storage for towels and toiletries.

NATURAL SURFACES. A combination of tumbled marble and natural stones covers the floor; black granite tops the tub deck and vanity counter.

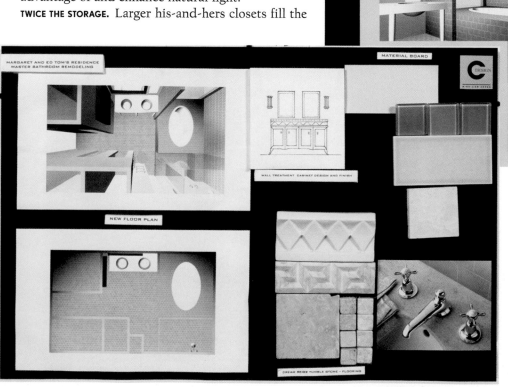

"The most important element in design is to create a space that satisfies the needs of the clients while complementing the architectural style of the house."

MINH-LIEN COHEN

2

DESIGNERS JEAN BLUMIN ASID & CAREN RIDEAU ASID, KITCHEN DESIGN GROUP

AT-HOME RETREAT. "The overall feeling for the Tom bath is to create an open space with a very relaxing feel, so that the couple can go in and retreat," Caren says. She and Jean propose an open layout with larger his-and-hers closets. Annexing an existing hall closet provides enough space for a whirlpool tub and a roomy steam shower, complete with drop-down teakwood seats. A new double vanity provides grooming space for both Ed and Margaret.

SEAMLESS DESIGN. To complement the architectural style of the Southern Colonial home, the designers suggest a dark wood vanity cabinet and pale limestone floors. Old-fashioned tile wainscoting covers the lower third of the walls; a soft pastel paint color covers the top two-thirds of the walls. Fixtures and faucets are vintage reproductions and include a soothing "rain" showerhead and a towel warmer.

LIGHT AND AIR. Ventilating windows are moved to maximize wall space; the windows are covered with vintage leaded-glass details to increase privacy.

"Our philosophy of design is to be very much in tune with the client. We are hands-on designers and always on-site to make sure each element works in harmony." JEAN BLUMIN

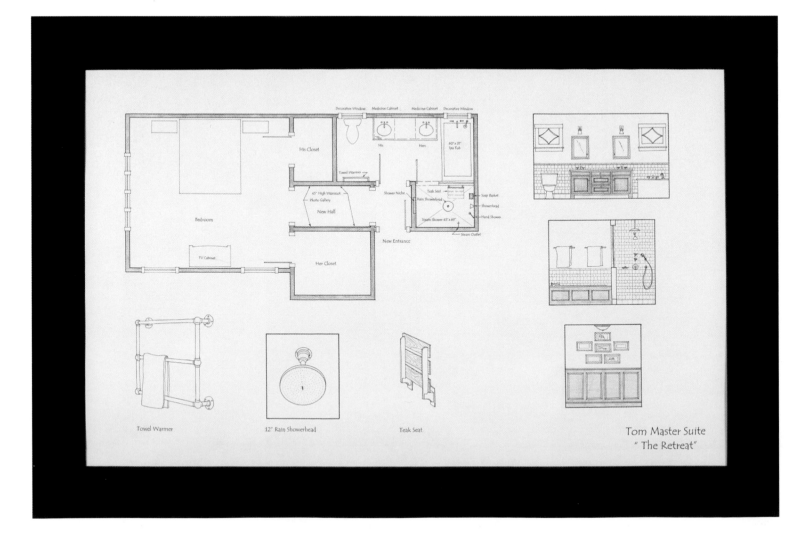

Towel Warmer

12" Rain Showerhead

Teak Seat

Tom Master Suite
"The Retreat"

3 DESIGNER MARY BROERMAN ASID, MDB DESIGN GROUP

ENHANCE A SMALL SPACE. "The Toms' master bath project is a challenge because it is in a traditional home in which the space is limited," Mary says. "The biggest challenge is to fit everything they want in the space they have." Her innovative layout provides enough space for a large whirlpool tub, a separate shower, and a private toilet room. "I created a whole new vanity area by moving the existing closets and creating one large walk-in instead," Mary says. "The new vanity has two sinks, each with its own medicine cabinet and with wall sconces on either side." A built-in storage tower fits between the two sinks.

SOMETHING NEW FROM SOMETHING OLD. The traditional styling of the new cherrywood vanity cabinet complements the other built-ins throughout the house. Tumbled travertine stone tiles cover the walls, and a complementary honed tile in a basket-weave pattern covers the floors. Existing windows remain in place but are trimmed with wall tile. Open shelves provide additional storage and display space for decorative accessories and toiletries.

"The design process is really two parts: One part is space planning, in which you develop the layout of the room, and the second part is the fun part, which is the interior design. When you have both parts working together, then your design is complete." MARY BROERMAN

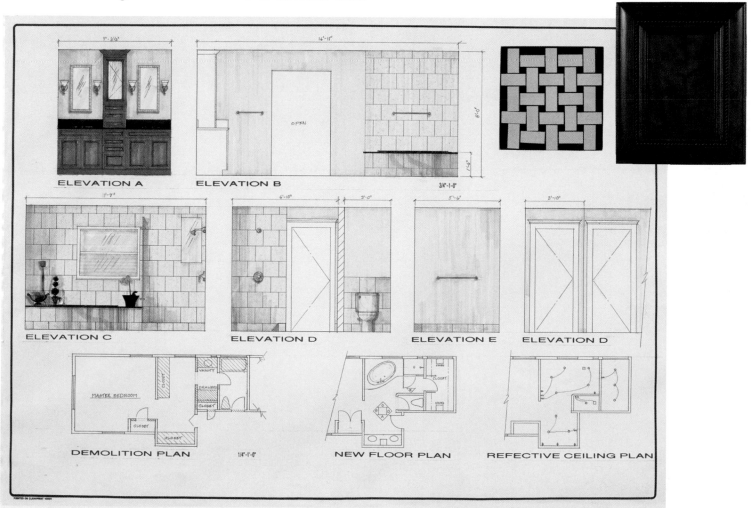

ELEVATION A   ELEVATION B

ELEVATION C   ELEVATION D   ELEVATION E   ELEVATION D

DEMOLITION PLAN   NEW FLOOR PLAN   REFECTIVE CEILING PLAN

"Minh-Lien's plan retains many of the architectural elements of our house and gives us the kind of space we have dreamt about for years," homeowner Ed Tom explains. "Now we feel like we're visiting a luxury spa without ever leaving home."

WHAT MAKES THIS PLAN WORK? Minh-Lien's design skillfully uses the existing square footage to create an open and airy master bath and keeps plumbing costs in check by keeping many of the plumbing lines in their original location. "Before the remodel, the bath felt small and cramped, and we felt like we were always in one another's way," Ed says. "Now the bath is a joy to share."

A custom-made vanity *opposite* provides his-and-hers sinks. The backsplash throughout the bath *above* is made of various decorative tiles. Perpendicular to the vanity, a new whirlpool tub *right* and glass-enclosed steam shower satisfy the couple's yearning for luxury hotel amenities. The tub offers a back massage, and a flat-panel TV mounted on the wall above the tub enables the couple to enjoy a massage while catching up on the day's events. The steam shower is large enough to sit in and unwind after a long day. Adjacent to the steam shower, a towel warmer offers another hotel luxury that even the Toms' two young children can't resist. "Everything in this bath is a treat," Ed says. "It's the perfect combination of form and function."

HOW CAN YOU GET THE LOOK? To make your bath feel like a getaway, include an amenity such as a steam shower or soaking tub that will help you relax and unwind. Splurge on a heated towel rack and thick towels so that you can wrap yourself in warmth at the beginning of every chilly morning. Adorn the walls and countertops with family photos and mementos so that you can begin and end every day in good spirits.

BEFORE THE MAKEOVER

If possible install extra light fixtures to make shaving and applying makeup easier. Attach a dimmer switch so that you can change the mood of the room at the touch of a button.

DID THE DESIGNER MEET THE BUDGET? Minh-Lien says she was able to meet the budget by laying out a design that enabled contractors to keep most of the plumbing lines in their original locations. Upgrades in fixtures caused a budget overage, but she says, "It enabled the Toms to get all the amenities they wanted, a trade-off they wanted to make." **ACTUAL COST** $43,000.

STONE SURFACES

Natural stone brings a warm and luxurious element into a bath. Its durability and ease-of-care make it an excellent surfacing choice in kitchens, baths, and any moisture-prone area. The tiles shown *left* are tumbled travertine in a basket-weave pattern with black granite inserts to match the vanity counter. Smooth, glossy stones, such as polished granite, can be slippery when wet; for better traction choose a honed finish. More porous varieties of stone, such as limestone, slate, and low-density marbles, are susceptible to staining and pitting and must be sealed periodically to prevent damage. Stone needs to be installed on a subsurface that does not give to prevent cracking.

BEFORE THE MAKEOVER

DETAILS MAKE THE DIFFERENCE. Dentil molding decorates the ceiling line *above* and matches molding treatments in the kitchen and living room. A new larger window at the end of the tub *opposite* mimics the style of the original windows in the home. Built from the same wood as the vanity, a small étagère *right* provides additional storage and display space for photos and perfumes.

1 ROOM 3 WAYS

designers'challenge

smart selections

As participants in HGTV's *Designers' Challenge*, the owners of the rooms featured throughout this book were privy to advice from design experts. In the end the chosen designer(s) guided owners through the process of selecting materials and finishes appropriate to their needs and lifestyles. Whether or not you plan to work with a professional, peruse these pages for the latest in appliances, flooring, countertops, and more—shown in more beautiful spaces. If you plan to hire an architect, designer, or a remodeling contractor, read Choosing Professionals on *page 184* to help you select a team who understands and shares your vision and will make your dreams a reality.

changethesurface To determine what flooring material will match your needs, think of what will work best in terms of wear and tear, cleanability, comfort, and style. Mix and match these popular and practical coverings to complement the activities performed in each room of your home.

CARPET   WOOD   STONE   LAMINATE

CARPET

Texture is the buzzword describing today's best-selling carpets, including uncut loop piles, which is how most berber carpets are made, and cut-pile friezes, where the individual tufts of yarn are clearly visible. Carpet weaves that combine cut- and loop-pile yarns to create sculptured effects as shown *above far left* are another popular choice. Longer cut piles that resemble the shag carpets of yesteryear are also making a comeback, but today's sturdier versions are less likely to tangle and mat.

The type of pile you choose does not affect wear, but the material you select does. Nylon is the most popular carpet material because it resists soiling and stains. Wool has a soft, cushy texture and wears nearly as well as nylon, but it may fade in strong sunlight. A wool/nylon blend combines the look and comfort of wool with the durability of nylon and costs less than pure wool. Other synthetic materials, such as acrylic, polyester, and olefin, may not wear as well as nylon or wool carpets. To determine weave quality, comparison-shop among brands by looking at the performance rating of the carpet. Performance ratings are based on the way the yarns are twisted (a tighter twist enhances durabil-

ity) and by the density of the tufts (the denser the better). Most carpets are rated on a 5-point scale, with a 4 or 5 rating being the best for high-traffic areas. Cost does not necessarily coincide with the ratings, so read the label of each sample.

WOOD

In addition to unfinished parquet tiles or wood planks that must be stained on-site, natural hardwoods are now available with prefinished urethane surfaces that provide higher scratch- and abrasion-resistance for extended wear than those previously available. Although seemingly more expensive than their unstained counterparts, the reduction in installation costs due to decreased labor make them a comparable buy. Like all wood, these prefinished floors are vulnerable to prolonged moisture.

CERAMIC TILE

Ceramic tile comes in more sizes and colors than any other flooring material, allowing you to create custom patterns. Durable, resistant to moisture, and generally low-maintenance, tile is a good choice for kitchens, mudrooms, and laundry areas. It can feel cold underfoot, especially in the bath against bare feet, but heating coils can be laid underneath to create warmth underfoot. Cost varies widely depending on the tiles you select and the complexity of the design and installation. Grout lines are susceptible to stains and can be difficult to keep clean. If possible choose darker grouts for high-traffic areas.

VINYL
A wide selection of colors and styles, including stone, tile, and hardwood look-alikes, makes this affordably priced resilient flooring a good choice for children's baths, play-rooms, and service areas. Available in tiles or 12- or 15-foot-wide rolls, pricing of the flexible flooring typically compares with quality; more expensive vinyls wear better and last longer.

VINYL   LINOLEUM   CORK

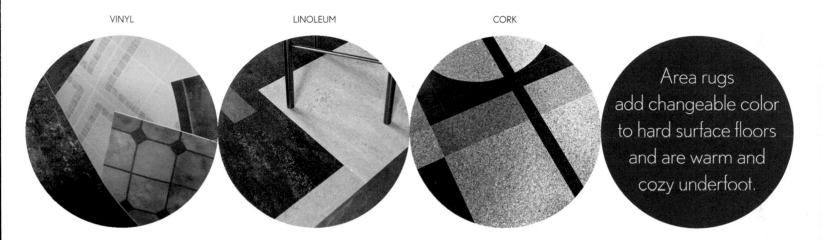

Area rugs add changeable color to hard surface floors and are warm and cozy underfoot.

STONE
Stone is an elegant flooring choice for entryways, master baths, kitchens, and great-rooms. Harder varieties like gran-ite require little maintenance and are nearly indestructible. Others, such as marble and limestone, are more porous and susceptible to staining, requiring sealing treatments. All stones tend to be expensive and, like ceramic tile, can feel cold to the touch. The surface can be warmed with heating coils laid underneath during installation.

LAMINATE
Today's laminates offer the look of wood, tile, and stone at a slightly lower price than the real thing. Available in strips and tiles, this hard surfacing material is durable, easy to clean, and requires little maintenance, but it cannot be refinished or restained (although individual planks can be replaced). Snap-together joints reduce installation time and make do-it-yourself projects a realistic alternative to paid professional installation. Some, but not all, laminates can be installed in areas where wood planks can't, such as in mois-ture-prone basements and children's baths.

LINOLEUM
Made from renewable resources, linoleum is more popular today than it was a decade ago. Unlike older styles, today's linoleums offer bright, lasting colors. Soft underfoot and a bit higher priced that vinyl, linoleum comes in both tile and sheet form and is easy to care for.

BAMBOO
Made from a stalky green plant and with a look that resem-bles hardwood, bamboo is becoming another popular floor-ing choice. Harder than maple and oak, the material also expands and contracts less. It is available both finished and unfinished, and it can be nailed or glued to a subfloor. Bamboo flooring is moderately high priced.

CORK
This resilient, cushioned surface is comfortable and quiet underfoot and moisture-resistant. Moderately high priced, the repairable flooring comes in tiles or planks and is made from renewable bark harvested from cork oak trees. It requires a urethane finish for easy sweeping and mopping.

changethesurface

Whether you are updating your kitchen, bath, playroom, or office, an ever-increasing array of countertop materials makes for innumerable design options, from standard laminate to contemporary concrete. Mix surfaces on islands and perimeter counters to match your functional requirements, style, and budget.

LAMINATE

A budget-priced, low-maintenance surface, plastic laminate offers an array of colors and patterns. Textures range from smooth and glossy to a mottled, leatherlike look. Some laminates resemble more expensive natural materials, such as stone or solid-surfacing. Resistant to grease and stains, laminate wipes clean with soap and water, but it can wear thin and dull over time. It is vulnerable to scratching, and hot pots can scorch the surface. Prolonged exposure to water may dissolve glue lines at seams and edges, causing the subsurface to warp.

CERAMIC TILE

Ceramic tile handles hot pans and curling irons without scorching. This surface is moisture-resistant and comes in a host of colors, patterns, and textures, making the decorating possibilities infinite. Some tiles mimic natural stone so perfectly that it is difficult to tell the difference. Prices vary greatly depending on the pattern selected. Tile grout, if left unsealed, can stain. To minimize discoloration, install a tiled countertop using narrow grout joints and a darker color grout. As with tile floors, price varies widely depending on the tiles you select and the complexity of the design and installation.

SOLID-SURFACING

Made from plastic resin, solid-surfacing countertops appear seam-free, require little maintenance, and are more durable than laminate. Priced comparably to most common stones (see *opposite* for more information), intense heat and heavy falling objects can cause damage to the material, but scratches and minor burns can be repaired with fine-grit sandpaper. A wide range of colors, patterns, and stone look-alikes are available. Edge treatments range from a simple smooth edge that imitates stone to intricate inlaid designs in contrasting colors. Solid-surfacing sinks can be integrated directly into the countertop, which means no seams to clean.

LAMINATE   CERAMIC TILE   SOLID-SURFACING   STAINLESS STEEL

STAINLESS STEEL

Stainless steel is the only other countertop material besides solid-surfacing that allows for one-piece countertop/sink formations. It withstands hot pots and pans and is easy to clean; however, it does show water spots and fingerprints and can be scratched by abrasive cleaners and sharp knives. Surface finishes range from a mirrorlike shine to a matte glow to complement a wide array of appliances and fixtures.

CONCRETE

Concrete is an increasingly popular countertop option because it can be colored, scored, and textured to create many interesting looks. Decorative tiles and metals can also be inlaid for a custom look. This material stands up well under heat, but because it is very porous, it must be sealed regularly for protection against stains. Hairline cracks are common but do not effect the strength of the material. Slabs can be poured on- or off-site. Prices vary greatly depending on installation requirements and the fabricator you choose.

STONE

Prized for natural beauty and durability, stone counters stand up to heat, water, and knives. Slabs are more expensive than stone tiles, but they eliminate grout cleanup. Ultrasmooth and cool, stone slabs are also ideal for kneading and rolling dough. Heavy falling objects can chip edges, but repairs are possible (although they may be noticeable). Granite is the least porous of the natural stones, making it one of the best choices for kitchen counters. Limestone and marble are more porous, so they must be sealed often to prevent staining and pitting. Specialty colors and patterns are more costly than more common varieties.

ENGINEERED QUARTZ

Made from crushed quartz and binders, engineered quartz has a composition, weight, and price comparable to granite. It is available in several colors and patterns that resemble mottled granite. Because it is nonporous, the material doesn't require sealants and is ideal for use in moisture-prone areas.

FAUX SLATE

This manufactured surface is often used in high school science labs and has no veins or feathers. The properties of faux slate are similar to those of a porous stone, so it is susceptible to staining, but it weighs and costs less than any of its natural counterparts.

BUTCHER BLOCK

Beautiful and durable, butcher-block counters are typically made from maple hardwood strips that are glued together. Periodic coats of oil help protect the wood from minor moisture damage. Shallow scratches and dents can be sanded and refinished. Sealants, when combined with routine care and thorough cleaning, make it a viable choice for many kitchen installations, but avoid using butcher block in moisture-prone areas.

> Decorative edge treatments add design dash, but they can double or triple the cost.

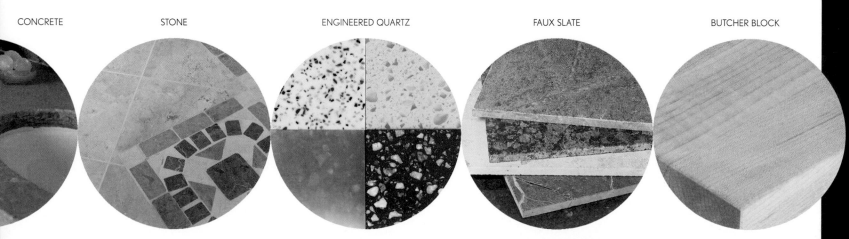

CONCRETE   STONE   ENGINEERED QUARTZ   FAUX SLATE   BUTCHER BLOCK

changethe**surface** Cabinetry can consume a large portion of a remodeling budget: as much as 40 percent of a kitchen renovation budget and 25 percent of a bath remodeling budget. Quality varies greatly between manufacturers and craftspeople, so select your cabinets carefully to ensure you get what you want—and what you pay for.

STOCK CABINETRY

Available for purchase from home centers and cabinetry retailers, these manufactured cabinets have improved in quality over the years and are now available in several different wood types and stain colors. Different manufacturers offer various colors and woods, but most large cabinetry companies offer oak, cherry, maple, pine, and birch. Reasonably priced storage options for stock cabinetry include recycling bins, clothes hampers, wine racks, drawer dividers, pasta bins, and plate racks. Furniturelike details include fretwork, carved inlays, and

glass doors— allowing you numerous opportunities to personalize your kitchen or bath at a price that's significantly less than custom.

Sizes are not as versatile as with semicustom or custom cabinets (they generally range from 15 inches wide to 48 inches wide in 3-inch increments) but you can often combine stock and semicustom cabinets to get the sizes and features your project requires. For kitchen cabinets the front-to-back depth usually runs 24 inches on base cabinets and 12 inches on wall cabinets. Base cabinets are typically 36 inches high; wall cabinet height varies. For baths, vanity cabinet front-to-back depth runs 18 to 21 inches; these cabinets are typically 29 to 30 inches high.

SEMICUSTOM CABINETRY

Like stock cabinets, these cabinets *opposite left* are available for purchase from cabinetry retailers; they have improved in quality over the years. This type of cabinetry also offers many details found in pricier custom cabinets. Every feature of stock cabinetry, from storage options to furniture details, is available in semicustom, but with a wider range of sizes—often as narrow as 9 inches. Heights and depths are comparable to stock cabinets. Wood species expand to include hickory and poplar, and more color and stain options are possible.

CUSTOM CABINETRY

These cabinets can be made to any specification to fit any space; heights and depths can meet individual comfort requirements as in the classic kitchen *opposite far left.*

CABINETRY TYPES

FACE-FRAME CABINETS. The framing of these cabinets attaches to the front of the cabinet box as shown in the office cabinetry *opposite left.* This type of construction is sturdy and results in a more traditional look. Drawers and pullouts are somewhat smaller than the overall cabinet dimensions because they must fit within the framing. As a result these cabinets offer less capacity than their frameless counterparts.

FRAMELESS CABINETS. These cabinets have door hinges that attach to the inside of the cabinet as shown in the kitchen *opposite far left* and on the cookie sheet storage cabinets *left.* They have a somewhat larger capacity than framed cabinets, but are more difficult to plan around and install because you must take into account door clearances when cabinets are installed at an angle or against a wall.

CABINETRY FRONTS

You can choose from three varieties:

FULL-INSET. These fronts are flush with the cabinet frame as shown in the kitchen *opposite far left.* These require excellent craftsmanship, so they are high priced and only available on custom cabinets.

PARTIAL-OVERLAY. These fronts conceal the opening but reveal some of the frame (see the office cabinetry *opposite left*). This style is affordable because it's easy to construct.

FULL-OVERLAY. These doors cover the entire box front. Slightly higher priced than partial overlays, these doors are not difficult to construct, but like frameless cabinets, door clearances must be considered when cabinets are installed at angles or against a wall.

JUDGING CABINET QUALITY

Take some time in a showroom to evaluate the quality of various cabinets. And ask a sales associate about the joints and materials used to construct the cabinets.

CONSTRUCTION MATERIALS. The cabinetry box is typically built from an engineered-wood panel, such as plywood, medium-density fiberboard (MDF), or particleboard. Plywood costs more than the other options but offers the best structural support.

JOINTS. Joints give cabinets their strength and stability; the better the joint, the better the cabinet. Butt joints that are stapled together are the least sturdy option. If possible choose cabinet boxes with front-to-back wood braces along the top edges of the sides and drawers that feature solid hardwood sides and dovetailed corner joints as shown in the drawer *left.*

Banks of drawers offer easier access and greater visibility than base cabinets fitted with fixed shelves.

changethe**surface** Today's appliances and fixtures are more attractive, functional, and energy-efficient than ever before. A host of functional innovations means faster cooking, easier cleanup, and greater durability. Here are the latest appliance and fixture innovations.

COOKTOPS & BURNERS

GAS. Traditional gas burners offer unsurpassed heat control, instant on and off, and economic operation. High-output and simmering burners increase heat control even further. Sealed gas burners contain spills and are easier to clean than traditional burners. Griddles and grills, available as options on high-price ranges, allow you to make grilled meats and veggies in your kitchen.

ELECTRIC. Ceramic glass cooktops feature special electric coils or instant-heat halogen elements under a smooth glass cooking surface. Because of their contemporary appearance and cleanability, they are gaining in popularity over traditional electric coils. Though affordably priced, they are higher priced than other electric models and can be more expensive to operate than their gas counterparts. Solid-disk electric burners have a solid cast-iron cooking surface that is a bit easier to clean and slightly higher priced than traditional coils. Traditional coil burners are available on value-priced models and are a tried-and-true favorite.

OVENS

TRADITIONAL THERMAL OVENS. Either gas or electric, these ovens use heating elements to roast, bake, and broil.

CONVECTION OVENS. Available as an option on both electric and dual-fuel ranges, these ovens use fans to circulate heated air around food for faster, more even cooking.

COMBINATION UNITS. Convection fans and microwave power combine for fast cooking with the browning of traditional thermal ovens.

CONVECTION STEAM OVENS. These ovens seal in nutrients, flavor, and color by circulating steam to consistently cook foods in 20 minutes or less. Steam cooking also defrosts and reheats without sacrificing moisture or flavor.

WARMING DRAWERS. Sized to fit standard cabinets, these electric

warmers *above* keep food hot and dinner plates warm.

PROGRAMMABLE REFRIGERATING OVENS. These ovens cool the oven compartment for up to 24 hours, then heat it up for cooking at whatever time you choose so that a meal is ready when you are.

VENTS

Vent fans are rated by how many cubic feet of air per minute (cfm) they move. For a conventional range, you need a fan rated from 200 to 300 cfm. Commercial ranges may require up to 1,500 cfm. For noise

control, choose a fan with a low sone rating. One sone, for example, is similar to a humming refrigerator. You can choose either an updraft or downdraft venting system.

UPDRAFT. These systems feature a hood that pulls air through a filter and ductwork leading to the outside

Today's trend, stainless-steel appliances, are available in nearly all price points.

and can help make the cooking area a focal point.

DOWNDRAFT. These systems either fit flush against a cooktop or rise above the countertop and draw out air through ductwork under the floor. Less conspicuous than venthoods, these vents are ideal to use with cooktops located in an island or peninsula.

DISHWASHERS

TRADITIONAL MODELS. Today's dishwashers offer lower sone ratings for quieter operation and sleek, easy-to-clean fronts with touch-pad controls. The door may be paneled to match cabinetry. Stainless-steel and lighted interiors are available as options on some models.

HIGH-CAPACITY MODELS. These dishwashers hold up to 20 percent more than standard models, but fit within the same space as standard models.

DISHWASHER DRAWERS. Often sold in pairs, one drawer takes up half the space of a traditional dishwasher. Run one to save water or two to separate china and cookware, or load and unload dishes in sequence.

REFRIGERATORS

Look for these new innovations in refrigeration when choosing a new model. Climate-controlled compartments extend the storage life of perishables. Icemakers located in the door free up freezer space. Optional glass door fronts require neatness, but enable you see items without warming the interior. Sealed and raised edges on glass shelves contain spills, while pullouts and adjustable shelves increase usable space and make cleaning easier. Side-by-side and drawer-size models *left* are accessible to people of a various heights and abilities. Refrigerated wine coolers *above* keep wines at the perfect temperature for longer storage and easier serving.

COFFEE BARS

Built-in coffeemakers and espresso machines are becoming a popular addition to both kitchens and baths. The programmable machines can be set so that the coffee is ready the moment your alarm clock rings. For the ultimate in cafe-style dining, install a warming drawer beneath the machine to keep cups and pastries warm.

SINKS

A wide selection of materials is available for sink basins, including stainless steel, enameled cast iron, vitreous china, quartz composite, solid-surfacing, soapstone, copper, and glass. Most of these materials are available in self-rimming and undermount styles; only metal and solid-surfacing sinks are available as an integrated bowl. Vessel sinks are available in a range of materials from metal to glass and often make the sink an architectural focal point.

SELF-RIMMING SINKS. The easiest sinks to install, self-rimming sinks come with a rim that overlays the countertop and holds the sink in place.

UNDERMOUNT SINKS. These sinks mount to the bottom of a stone or solid-surfacing countertop, making cleanup easy because there is no rim on which crumbs can catch.

INTEGRATED SINKS. Sinks and countertops are made of one seamless material for easy cleanup.

APRON-FRONT SINKS. As shown *far right* these vintage farm-style sinks have a decorative front called an apron that transforms a cleanup area into a decorative focal point.

VESSEL SINKS. As shown *right* these sinks resemble free-standing bowls and are available in most any color and size.

FAUCETS & SHOWERHEADS

Chrome faucets are still staples, but they've been joined by a host of other metals as well as powder-coated epoxy in an array of colors. Washerless and ceramic disk valves have replaced rubber washers. Pullout wands, handheld showerheads, body sprays, pot-fillers, instant hot and cold water, and water-filtering systems are all available options.

TOILETS

Design choices range from classic two-pieces models to low-profile one-piece units. Models with elongated bowls are more comfortable for most users but are typically more expensive. Toilets range in height from 14 to 17 inches; taller toilets are more comfortable for people over 6 feet tall and for people with disabilities.

The latest technological advances increase flushing suction and reduce noise.

SHOWERS

There are three basic types of shower stalls:

PREFABRICATED STALLS. Affordably priced and available in a variety of shapes and colors, one-piece, two-piece, and three-piece versions fit most new construction or remodeling applications. Fiberglass with a finish surface of acrylic creates a sturdier stall than solid plastic models. Doors and curtains are typically sold separately.

PREFABRICATED PANS. These molded, waterproof floor covers are available in a range of materials from plastic to stone. They can be combined with prefabricated shower walls or custom-made stone, ceramic tile, or solid-surfacing walls.

CUSTOM-MADE STALLS. These stalls offer the most design flexibility; there's no limit to the size or the style of a custom-made shower. Any waterproof material or combination of materials can be used, including ceramic tile, marble, granite, solid-surfacing, tempered glass, and glass blocks.

TUBS

As with sinks, bathtubs are made from materials such as enameled cast iron, enameled steel, fiberglass finished with acrylic or another plastic, and cast polymer—a tub made of solid-surfacing which resembles natural stone. Both whirlpool and standard tubs come in four basic designs.

RECESSED TUBS. With one finished side called an apron, a recessed tub

fits between two end walls and against a back wall.

CORNER TUBS. These space-saving tubs fit diagonally between two corners and have only one finished side. Some corner tubs have a finished side and a finished end or a curved side so that they can be installed parallel to one wall.

FREESTANDING TUBS. These tubs are finished on all fours sides and can be placed anywhere that you can run plumbing lines. Both contemporary-style and old-fashioned claw-foot models are available.

PLATFORM TUBS. Similar to a self-rimming sink, these tubs have no finished sides and may be dropped into a custom platform made to fit the tub in a material of your choice.

CUSTOM TUBS. As with showers, custom-made tubs can be made from ceramic tile, solid-surfacing, marble, and granite to fit any spaces of any size.

LIGHTING

For the most effective interior lighting, choose a combination of ambient, task, and accent lighting.

AMBIENT. Also called general or overall lighting, ambient lighting mimics sunlight, enabling you to see from one side of the room to the other. Chandeliers, track lights, and ceiling-mounted fixtures are all sources of ambient lighting. As a general guideline, provide at least 1,700 lumens (the light output generated by a 100-watt incandescent lightbulb or a 25-watt fluorescent) for each 50 square feet of floor space.

TASK. As the name implies, this light illuminates a specific work or grooming area. Reading, cooking, and applying makeup all require strong, direct light. To generate task lighting, choose such fixtures as pendant lights as shown in the kitchen *left*, table lamps, or recessed lights that focus light in one area. For reading and writing, the diameter of the beam spread should be at least 16 inches. Overlap these beams on larger work surfaces, such as a kitchen island or a sewing table. To light grooming mirrors in vanity areas, make sure the light is even and free of shadows. If possible choose a light-color countertop so that more light reflects up on your face.

ACCENT. This light makes a room sparkle. Illuminating artwork with spotlights or wall sconces, adding uplights above built-in cabinetry or on a soffit as shown *above*, or lining a tub with a row of lit candles are a few ways to add accent lighting.

changethe**surface** Give your home a fresh face with beautiful windows, doors, and decorative moldings. Match design details, such as window muntins and door casings, to those existing in your home and your new additions will look like stylish originals.

WINDOWS

New sizes, shapes, and grid designs can make windows some of the most attractive features in your home.
INNOVATIVE FEATURES. Retractable window screens roll up and out of sight when not in use. Insulated glazing and special coatings on the glass make many windows more energy efficient and reduce fading on interior fabrics. Exterior surfaces—typically vinyl or aluminum—never need painting. Concealed latches combine with a wide range of colors, enabling you to customize windows to match your design scheme and architectural style. Price tends to increase with style; custom

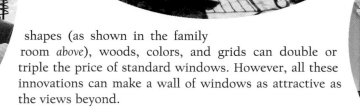

shapes (as shown in the family room *above*), woods, colors, and grids can double or triple the price of standard windows. However, all these innovations can make a wall of windows as attractive as the views beyond.

DOORS

Like windows, doors are also becoming functional focal points. Material choices range from solid hardwood to mahogany and Douglas fir to insulated steel and fiberglass. Decorative glass panels let in light and can be frosted to obscure the view and keep privacy intact. Sliding pockets that disappear into the wall are good choices for small interior passageways. French doors draw attention to door openings and enable light to filter from adjoining rooms or exteriors. In the dining room *below*, pairs of glass doors combine with muntin-divided transoms to create the illusion of dining alfresco.

ARCHITECTURAL MOLDINGS

Give your home architectural appeal with stock moldings as those shown *bottom left*, which are available at home centers and lumberyards.

CHAIR RAILS. Located about a third of the way up a wall, these moldings protect the walls from chair dings—ideal additions for dining rooms, family rooms, and sitting areas.

PICTURE MOLDINGS. These moldings are applied to the wall a foot or two below the ceiling and provide a spot from which pictures can be hung. Use them in rooms where you plan to showcase oil paintings, wall colors, or framed prints.

CROWN AND BASEBOARD MOLDINGS. These decorative trims create interest where walls meet ceilings and floors. Choose widths and designs that complement the style of your room, or combine and layer moldings to create a focal point as shown on the fireplace mantel *below*. Most moldings attach to the wall with finishing nails and carpenter glue and can be purchased either prefinished or ready-to-finish so you can customize them to match your decor.

To take advantage of changing light throughout the day, place windows on two sides of every room.

choosingprofessionals

Choosing the best professionals to design and execute your decorating or remodeling project will make your entire experience more enjoyable and ensure top-notch results. Whether you're searching for an architect, an interior designer, or a remodeling contractor, you can use these tactics to track down the ones who share your vision.

GATHER

Collect the names of professionals to investigate and interview. Ask friends and colleagues for suggestions and recommendations. Identify local referrals with the help of professional organizations, such as the American Institute of Architects (AIA), 800-242-3837, website: aia.org; the National Association of Home Builders Remodelers Council (NAHB), 800-368-5242 ext. 8216, website: nahb.com; the National Association of the Remodeling Industry (NARI) 800-611-6274, website: nari.org; or the American Society of Interior Designers (ASID), 202-546-3480, website: asid.org. These websites can help you find a contractor in your area: handymanonline.com; improvenet.com; remodelnet.com; and homeownersreferral.com.

EXPLORE

Call the professionals on your list—you should have four or five from each profession—and ask for references. Contact the clients they name and ask them to recount their positive and negative experiences. Also, if you've seen a recent decorating or remodeling project that you like, contact the homeowners and ask about their experience and results.

EVALUATE

Based on these references, interview your top three choices and tour some of their finished projects. Savvy architects and contractors will ask you questions as well to determine your expectations and needs. You should come away from each interview and tour with an idea of the quality of their work and how well your personalities and visions for the project match.

SOLICIT

To narrow your choices, it may be worth the additional cost to solicit preliminary drawings from each professional. This is a great way to test your working relationship and to gather options from which to choose—as shown in each room featured in this book and on the *Designers' Challenge* show. Also ask contractors for bids. Don't base your decision on cost alone, but weigh what you learned in the interview with the thoroughness of the bid itself.

SIGN UP

Before beginning a project with any professional, have the facts on paper to legally protect you before, during, and after the work is done. Define the scope of the project and fees as specifically as possible. The contract should include a clear description of the work to be done, materials that will be required, and who will supply them. It should also spell out commencement and completion dates, any provisions relating to timeliness, and your total costs (subject to additions and deductions by a written change order only). Payments should be tied to work stages; be wary of any contractor who wants a lot of money up front. If ordering certain materials needs to be done weeks in advance (to allow time for manufacturing), get a list of all those materials and their cost before committing to up-front money. Kitchens, for example, may require a sizable cash advance to finance appliances and cabinetry. If possible make out these initial checks to the subcontractors and retailers directly.

SURVIVAL TIPS

When your home transforms into a construction zone, the mess can make you wonder if your life will ever be back to normal. To ensure the minor inconveniences of a decorating makeover or a remodeling project don't become major headaches, discuss cleanup with your contractor before work begins. Have a team meeting with all the key professionals and ask for an overview of the entire project so that together you can develop a plan to minimize disruption.

ASK WORKERS TO ARRIVE AND LEAVE AT REASONABLE HOURS. Noise is inevitable. Understand that if you set shorter workdays, you will also be setting, and possibly lengthening, the duration of the project. Let the contractor know in advance if there are any times, such as holidays or special family events, when your house will be off-limits.

SET UP "TEMPORARY ROOMS." If you're remodeling the kitchen, for example, move the refrigerator, the coffee pot, and the microwave to the dining room. If you're remodeling more than one bath, ask for a timeline that keeps one of the baths in service until the next one is ready to use again. If you don't want workers to use your restrooms, set up a portable toilet near the entrance to the remodeling area.

BE FLEXIBLE. No matter how meticulously you schedule your project, there is bound to be a surprise or two. Go with the flow and be willing to change out a discontinued fabric, tile, or fixture.

PROFESSIONAL AFFILIATIONS

Many interior design and remodeling professionals have acronyms or abbreviations listed behind their name. Like the letters MD behind a doctor, these designations refer to some specific educational requirements the professional has met as well as his or her membership in a professional organization that provides additional training or testing. Here is what the most common abbreviations—present throughout this book—mean.

AIA. American Institute of Architects. AIA members are required to be a licensed architect (in most states, this means six or seven years of education followed by a one- to two-year internship and the passing of a licensing exam). They also must follow a strict code of professional ethics and take at least 18 hours of continuing education per year.

AKBD. Associate Kitchen and Bath Designer. AKBDs must have at least two years of experience or an equivalent of experience and education, pass an AKBD examination, and attend at least 30 hours of NKBA professional development programs (see *right*).

ASID. American Society of Interior Designers. Membership requirements vary from state to state, but all require a combination of accredited design education and/or full-time work experience and passing a two-day accreditation examination administered by the NCIDQ (see *right*). Continuing education credits are needed to retain the accreditation. Allied ASID members meet all the educational requirements, but have not taken the NCIDQ examination.

CBD. Certified Bath Designer. CBDs must have at least seven years of experience or an equivalent of experience and education specializing in residential bathroom design and installation. They must also pass a seven-hour examination administered by the NKBA (see *below*). CBDs are required to submit affidavits of professional competence from industry professionals and clients to the NKBA. To retain the accreditation, designers must continue their industry education and actively participate in NKBA programs.

CID. Certified Interior Designer. CIDs must pass a state licensing exam. They follow the laws of that particular state regarding interior design consultation.

CKD. Certified Kitchen Designer. Like CBDs, CKDs must have at least seven years of experience or an equivalent of experience and education specializing in the design and installation of residential kitchens, pass a similar exam, and meet the same competency requirements.

CMKBD. Certified Master Kitchen and Bath Designer. CMKBDs must have 10 years of kitchen and bath industry experience in addition to the experience demonstrated for CKD and CBD certifications as administered by the NKBA.

IDS. Interior Design Society. Professional members must have successfully completed the Council for Qualification of Residential Interior Designers (CQRID) examination; or hold a valid legal registration in interior design by the state in which the applicant's principal office or place of business is located; or hold professional membership in another design association recognized by the IDS.

IIDA. International Interior Design Association. IIDA professional members are part of a worldwide association of interior designers. Professional members must pass the NCIDQ and are required to take 10 hours of continuing education every two years.

NCIDQ CERTIFIED. This certification means the professional has taken and passed the examination required by the ASID. The exam is administered by the National Council for Interior Design Qualification (NCIDQ).

NKBA. National Kitchen and Bath Association. This association administers tests (as stated *above*) and offers professional development courses for kitchen and bath designers. It also offers consumers resources for selecting professionals and budgeting (website: nkba.org).

> Choose professionals who have experience with projects of the same size and complexity as yours.

designers&resources

To see more rooms designed by many of the professionals listed below, visit HGTV.com/designers.

PAGES 12-19, COMFORT FOR A CROWD, EPISODE 820

DESIGNERS. Jackie Filtzer Bayer and Jessica Glynn, Merchandising East, Ellicott City, Maryland; 410-465-2440; *e-mail:* jackie@merchandisingeast.com or jessie@merchandisingeast.com; *website:* merchandisingeast.com. Lindsay Flower, Ann Lindsay Interiors, Inc.; 410-337-9348; *e-mail:* info@annlindsayinteriors.com. Victor Liberatore, Victor Liberatore Interior Design; 410-444-6942, toll-free: 866-474-0036; *e-mail:* victorliberatore@aol.com; *website:* victorliberatoreinteriordesign.com.

PHOTOGRAPHER. Gordon Beall

RESOURCES. *Furniture:* Stroheim & Romann Showroom; 202-484-4562; fax: 202-554-0153; *e-mail:* info@stroheim.com; *website:* stroheim.com. *Fireplace mantel and custom furniture:* Bayne's Quality Custom Furniture Inc.; 410-945-8313; *e-mail:* mail@baynesfurniture.com; *website:* baynesfurniture.com. *Carpeting:* CB Flooring; 410-290-7770; *website:* cbflooring.com. *Faux finishing:* Paint Designs; 410-267-0657. *Custom draperies:* Sew Business; 410-875-2327; *e-mail:* sjh1529@aol.com. *Floral supplies and design:* Foxglove; 410-244-1369; *website:* foxglovedesign.com.

PAGES 20-29, ROOM WITH A VIEW, EPISODE 724

DESIGNERS. Constance Ramos, Ramos Design Consultants, 2905A Sepulveda Blvd. #120, Manhattan Beach, CA 90266; 310-546-6317; *e-mail:* constanceramos@adelphia.net; *website:* ramos-design.com. James Swan, James Swan and Company, Inc.; 310-659-3488; *e-mail:* jim@jamesswanco.com; *website:* jamesswanco.com. Charlie Platero Jr., Charlie Platero Jr. Interior Design; 661-272-0734; fax: 661-267-6883; *e-mail:* charlieplaterojr@hotmail.com.

PHOTOGRAPHER. Edmund Barr

RESOURCES. *Handblown and sculpted glass:* McQuaid Art Glass; 949-497-8753; *e-mail:* mcquaidart@earthlink.net; *website:* mcquaidartglass.com. *Furniture:* The Designer Sofa Factory; 310-559-9901; *e-mail:* peter@designersofafactory.com *and* Patrick H. Lennon Woodworking; 310-640-1828. *Decorative painting:* Manhattan Painting Company; 310-545-5722; *e-mail:* manhattanpainting@earthlink.com. *Window coverings:* Rayson Window Coverings; 310-379-1196; *e-mail:* info@raysonwindowcoverings.com; *website:* raysonwindowcoverings.com. *Stone and tile:* American International Stone & Tile; 310-937-5830; *e-mail:* americanstone@cs.com.

PAGES 30-39, SMALL SPACES, SMART STYLE, EPISODE 822

DESIGNERS. Sue Gorman, Sue Gorman Interior Designs; 714-505-0639; *e-mail:* information@suegormaninteriors.com; *website:* suegormaninteriors.com. Beth Whitlinger, Beth Whitlinger Interior Design, A Division of the J.E.W.L., L.L.C.; 949-766-1093; fax: 949-766-1092; *e-mail:* bwhitlinger@cox.net; *website:* bethwhitlinger.com. Shawn Hayes, Hayes Interior Design; 714-771-6973; fax: 714-771-5773; *e-mail:* chayes2@socal.rr.com.

PHOTOGRAPHER. Edmund Barr

RESOURCES. *Custom ironwork:* Pacifica Iron; 714-424-9092; fax: 714-424-9095. *Upholstery fabric:* Kravet Fabrics; *website:* kravet.com. *Pillows:* Unique Quilting; 714-258-0311; fax: 714-258-0328. *Furniture:* JDM/Juhasz, Inc.; 323-731-6789; fax: 323-731-1004; *e-mail:* jdmjuhasz@att.net; *website:* juhaszdesign.com *and* Joseph Christian Showroom, 949-831-1835; fax: 949-831-8693. *Art and custom framing:* Westervelt's Fine Art; 949-643-1720; fax: 949-643-0255. *Stone and tile:* Surface Concepts; 949-348-1088; fax: 949-348-1089; *e-mail:* surfaceconcepts@cox.net. *Slate tile:* Jolanta Tile; 714-937-5225. *Faux finishing:* John Trainor, 949-218-1963; fax: 949-218-1963. *Lighting:* Hubbardton Forge; 802-468-3090; fax: 802-468-3284; *e-mail:* info@vtforge.com; *website:* vtforge.com. *Custom murals:* Mural Man, 714-521-1711, *website:* mural-man.com. *Accessories:* Mikim Home Collection; 714-966-6622; fax: 714-966-6627; De Benedictis; 949-831-9411; fax: 949-831-9044 *and* Furniture and Accessory showroom; 714-549-1442.

PAGES 40-47, FINE FRENCH LIVING, EPISODE 717

DESIGNERS. Sandy Craig and Christy Hopple, Ryan Taylors Interior Design; 714-256-7730; fax: 714-256-7733. Cassandra Kreps, Cassandra Kreps Interior Design and Design Specialty, LLC; 323-691-8033; *e-mail:* ckdesign@aol.com. Miguel Angel Zavala, Found Gallery; 323-467-0966; *e-mail:* foundgallery@aol.com.

PHOTOGRAPHER. Edmund Barr

RESOURCES. *Piano:* Keyboard Concepts; 310-586-5588. *Lighting:* Uni-Lite; 714-991-0710. *Area rugs:* Pacific Looms; 949-585-9019; *website:* pacificlooms.com. *Fabric:* Robert Allen, Pacific Design Center; 310-659-6454; *website:* robertallendesign.com *and* Fabricut Fabrics: toll-free: 800-999-8200; *website:* fabricut.com. *Wall coverings:* TRI-KES Wallcovering Source; *website:* trikes.com.

PAGES 48–55, EVERYDAY WORK & PLAY, EPISODE 825

DESIGNERS. Lauren Jacobsen, Jacobsen Design; 818-763-2555; fax: 818-763-0586; *e-mail:* lauren@Ljacobsendesign.com; *website:* Ljacobsendesign.com.
Charlie Platero Jr., Charlie Platero Jr. Interior Design; 661-272-0734; fax: 661-267-6883; *e-mail:* charlieplaterojr@hotmail.com.
Kenneth Dean and Shayna Bell, Dean International Designs; 661-251-0170.

PHOTOGRAPHER. Edmund Barr

RESOURCES. *Rug:* Designer's Home Accent/Designer's Rug Warehouse; 310-632-5510; *website:* designersrugwarehouse.com.

PAGES 56–63, CLASSIC & KID-FRIENDLY, EPISODE 917

DESIGNERS. Suzan Decker Ross and Janet Marie Thomas, Decker Ross Interiors, 936-C Cleveland St., Clearwater, FL 33755; 727-442-9996; fax: 727-442-1935, *e-mail:* suzan@deckerross.com; *website:* deckerross.com.
Richard E. Carle, Chateau Designs, Inc., 2566 McMullen-Booth Rd., Ste. E, Clearwater, FL 33771; 727-726-2243; fax: 727-726-0157; *e-mail:* recdesign@aol.com.
Susan Taylor and Connie Rhodes, Taylor Designs Unlimited, Inc.; 5500 Central Ave., St. Petersburg, FL 33707; 727-343-6208; fax: 818-764-2869; *e-mail:* susan.taylor@worldnet.att.net.

PHOTOGRAPHER. Dick Dickinson

RESOURCES. *Tile and marble:* Suncoast Tile & Marble; 727-585-6914. *Paint:* Porter Paints; 727-446-9114; *website:* porterpaints.com. *Stained glass:* The Stained Glass Company; 727-785-4291; fax: 727-785-4291. *Rugs:* Carillon Carpet; 727-442-9538; fax: 727-447-3655; *website:* carillonrugs.com and D&D Designs; 818-806-0706; fax: 818-806-0705. *Cabinets:* Kraftmaid Cabinetry; toll-free: 888-562-7744; *website:* kraftmaid.com. *Custom furnishings:* Harden House; 727-442-7546; fax: 727-445-9537; *e-mail:* thehardenhouse@aol.com. *Furniture hardware:* Cobblestone Court; 727-799-8608; fax: 727-799-2329.

PAGES 64–71, PRETTY & PET-FRIENDLY, EPISODE 725

DESIGNERS. Diane Kolesar, Ethan Allen; 310-534-0904; fax: 310-534-0842; *e-mail:* dianethek@aol.com; *website:* ethanallen.com.
Eric Guenther, Glabman's Furniture and Interior Design; 949-388-9600; *e-mail:* erguenther@aol.com; *website:* glabman.com/refurbished furnishings.
Janie Bowers, Janie Bowers Interior Design; 310-328-8690; *e-mail:* jbowers1@socalrr.com; *website:* janiebowers.com.

PHOTOGRAPHER. Edmund Barr

RESOURCES. *Refurbished furnishings:* Not Too Shabby; 310-376-5200; *website:* nottooshabbydecor.com. *Window coverings:* Hunter Douglas Window Fashions; toll-free: 800-937-7895; *e-mail:* consumer@hunterdouglas.com. *website:* hunterdouglas.com. *Decorative project materials:* Fashion Tech; *website:* fashiontech.com. *Room furnishings:* Ethan Allen; 203-743-8000; *website:* ethanallen.com.

PAGES 72–81, CLASSIC & CASUAL, EPISODE 805

DESIGNERS. Brigette Boyd, Brigette Boyd Interiors; 714-679-0117; *e-mail:* designingwoman@cox.net.
Sue Gorman, Sue Gorman Interior Designs; 714-505-0639; *e-mail:* information@suegormaninteriors.com; *website:* suegormaninteriors.com.
Kelly J. Kelter, Details Design; 714-960-6619; fax: 714-536-6693.

PHOTOGRAPHER. Edmund Barr

RESOURCES. *Natural stone:* Marmol Export; 714-939-0697; fax: 714-939-1401; *e-mail:* Tugboat4007@hotmail.com. *Furniture:* Images; 714-379-8815; fax: 714-379-8816; *e-mail:* Imagesfurnishings@verizon.net; *website:* images-furnishings.com and Maureen's Country Specialties; 207-793-4398; *e-mail:* Mpc4@adelphia.net; *website:* maureenscountryspecialties.com. *Audio/video and home-theater electronics:* Audio Video Today; 714-891-7575; fax: 714-893-8835; *website:* audiovideotoday.com. *Furniture and accessories:* Exposures; toll-free: 800-222-4947; fax: 888-345-3702; *website:* exposuresonline.com. *Decorative project materials:* Artistry In Metal; 714-897-9144. *Leaded-glass sidelights and transom:* R.D. Gibbs & Co. Inc.; 818-249-1509; fax: 818-249-1719. *Smoke chamber cabinet reproduction:* V.W. Steeber Construction Company; 562-818-6071; fax: 562-590-3224. *Side table and candleholder:* Michael Gatlin; 714-841-9666.

PAGES 82–91, FAMILY LIVING & DINING, EPISODE 802

DESIGNERS. Annie Speck, Annie Speck Interior Designs; 949-464-1957; fax: 949-464-1947; *e-mail:* annie@anniespeck.com; *website:* anniespeck.com.
Linda Lansford, Linda Lansford Interior Design; 949-721-0772; fax: 949-721-0752; *e-mail:* lansch@sbcglobal.net.
Sally Ketterer, Sally Ketterer Interiors; 949-733-2955; fax: 949-733-0766; *e-mail:* designers4@juno.com.

PHOTOGRAPHER. Edmund Barr

RESOURCES. *Custom furniture:* Mario Grimaldi International; 323-778-9639; fax: 323-778-4829; *website:* mgrimaldi.com. *Drapery construction:* Ramos Design; 818-761-9246. *Hardwood flooring:* AGF Hardwood; toll-free: 800-665-6003. *Upholstery fabric:* Kravet Fabrics; *website:* kravet.com. *Upholstered furniture:* Chair Choice; 626-969-9906. *Lighting:* Allied Lighting; 949-646-3737. *Faux finishing:* Decorative Finishes and Coatings; 949-548-1840.

PAGES 92–99, LOFTY EXPECTATIONS, EPISODE 916

DESIGNERS. Terri Main, Main Design Innovations; 248-231-4969; fax: 248-588-1270.
Barbi Krass, Colorworks Studio; 248-851-7540; fax: 248-851-7884; *e-mail:* barbi@colorworksstudio.com; *website:* colorworksstudio.com.
Ellen Premtaj, Elle Interiors; 313-682-0006; fax: 313-383-5389; *e-mail:* epremtaj@aol.com.

PHOTOGRAPHER. Beth Singer

RESOURCES. *Custom furniture:* Scott Brazeau Metal Furniture; 248-335-3980; fax: 248-542-4152 *and* Janet's Upholstery; 248-426-0236; fax: 248-426-0237. *Solar shades:* McDonald Wholesale Distributing, Inc; 313-273-2870; fax: 313-273-8030. Carpet: Masland; 800-633-0468; *website:* maslandcarpets.com. *Furniture:* Carter's Furniture; 704-633-8000; fax: 704-637-2851. *Fabric:* Knoll Textiles; 800-343-3480. *Dining table:* Surface Concrete; 313-874-5922; fax: 313-874-5933. *Furniture:* Thayer Coggin; 336-841-6000; fax: 336-841-3245. *Custom cabinetry:* ECS Cabinetry; 248-624-0800; fax: 248-676-2834. *Paint:* The Sherwin-Williams Company; *website:* sherwin.com.

PAGES 102–109 VACATION 24/7, EPISODE 807

DESIGNERS. Annie Walton-Teter, Studio Annik; 310-392-4246; fax: 310-392-3119; *e-mail:* awt@annik.org; *website:* studioannik.com.
Ron Hunt, Haven Grove Design Group L.L.C.; 818-951-7620; fax: 818-951-7619; *e-mail:* havengrove@aol.com.
Kim Scherzi, Porta Bella; 310-820-2550; fax: 310-820-1840; *e-mail:* kascherzi@hotmail.com.

PHOTOGRAPHER. Edmund Barr

RESOURCES. *Architectural and decorative glass:* UltraGlas, Inc.; 818-772-7744; toll-free: 800-777-2332; *website:* ultraglas.com.

PAGES 110–117, ASIAN BATH OASIS, EPISODE 902

DESIGNERS. Michelle Kaufmann, MK Architecture; 415-999-4122; *e-mail:* michelle@mkarchitecture.com; *website:* mkarchitecture.com.
Camille Urban Jobe, Urban Jobe Architecture; 512-585-3466; *e-mail:* cjobe@urbanjobe.com; *website:* urbanjobe.com.
Yvonne Lane Wonder, Yvonne Lane Interior LLC; 415-454-3292; fax: 415-454-3293; *e-mail:* yvonne@yvonnelaneinteriors.com; *website:* yvonnelaneinteriors.com.
Albert Carey, Lamperti Associates; 415-454-1623; fax: 415-454-2385; *e-mail:* lmprtiasso@aol.com; *website:* lampertiassociates.com.

PHOTOGRAPHER. Edmund Barr

RESOURCES. *Custom woodwork:* Out of the Woods; 415-457-0647; *e-mail:* info@outofthewoods.cc; *website:* outofthewoods.cc. *Kitchen and bath fixtures:* Kohler Company, toll-free: 800-456-4537; *e-mail:* info@kohler.com; *website:* kohler.com. *Custom doors and windows:* Santa Clara Lumber & Millwork; 408-241-8777. *Tile:* Import Tile Co.; 510-843-5744. *Custom glass art:* Nikolas Weinstein Studios; 415-643-5418; *e-mail:* info@nikolas.net; *website:* nikolas.net. *Custom art:* Chris Stokes; *website:* cwstokes.com.

PAGES 118–125, OLD-WORLD ACCENTS, EPISODE 722

DESIGNERS. Barry Korn, Creative Kitchen Design; 310-836-7893; fax: 310-836-6773; *e-mail:* barrykorn@yahoo.com.
Ron Woodson, Ron Woodson Fine Art and Design; 323-644-3322; fax: 323-667-1187; *website:* ronwoodsondesign.com.
Dolores Esparza, Dolores Esparza Interior and Architectural Designs; 626-570-9936; fax: 626-570-9936.

PHOTOGRAPHER. Edmund Barr

RESOURCES. *Bathroom sinks:* Rohl Corporation; 714-557-1933; *website:* rohlhome.com. *Bathroom faucets:* Concinnity; *website:* concinnityusa.com. *Malibu tile:* California Pottery & Tile Works; 323-235-4151; *website:* malibutile.com. *Granite counters:* Color Marble; 626-308-0802; *website:* colormarble.com

PAGES 126–133, HOTEL SUITE RETREAT, EPISODE 719

DESIGNERS. Karen Began, KB Designs; 805-383-1151; fax: 805-484-3959; *e-mail:* kbdsn@aol.com.
Jone Pence, Jone Pence Interior Design & Construction; 805-644-2188; fax: 805-644-0747; *e-mail:* jonepencedesign@sbcglobal.net; *website:* jonepencedesign.com.
Linda Evarts and Jeremy Evarts, Mark's Carpet & Design; 805-658-8444; fax: 805-658-9034; *website:* markscarpet.com.

PHOTOGRAPHER. Edmund Barr

RESOURCES. *Light fixtures:* Lights Beautiful; 805-643-0883; fax: 805-643-5281; *e-mail:* lbbs1@msn.com. *Building materials:* Terry Sash & Door; 818-881-8738. *Custom furniture:* Santa Monica Millworks; 310-393-6775; fax: 310-395-3675; *e-mail:* Memo@smmillworks.com. *Furniture:* Palecek; toll-free: 800-274-7730; *e-mail:* info@palecek.com; *website:* palecek.com. *Accessories:* Palermo; 805-643-3070; fax: 805-643-3011. *Fabric:* Duralee Fabrics; 310-360-0778. *Window hardware:* Kirsch, a division of Newell Rubbermaid; toll-free: 800-538-6567; *e-mail:* info@kirsch.com; *website:* kirsch.com. *Fabric and furniture:* Kravet Showroom; 310-659-7100; fax: 310-657-4029; *website:* kravet.com. *Carpeting:* Isensee Floorcovering, Inc.; 805-648-5333; fax: 805-648-5127. *Paint:* ICI Paints, toll-free: 800-627-1650; *e-mail:* icipaintsstores@ici.com; *website:* icipaintstores.com. *Artwork:* Wendy Lefkowitz; 805-642-4619;

e-mail: rblefko@avenuecable.com *and* Nora Stewart;
805-653-5634; *e-mail:* norastewart@earthlink.net.
Frames: Artwork Services; 805-643-4399; fax: 805-643-0071.

PAGES **134–143**, CONTINUITY WITH COMFORT, EPISODE **720**

DESIGNERS. Janet Bussell and Barrie Livingstone,
Bussell Livingstone Interiors, Inc.; 310-317-9642;
e-mail: barrie@blinteriors.com; janet@blinteriors.com;
website: blinteriors.com.
Pamela Munson, Munson & Company, Inc.;
818-563-1442; *e-mail:* pamunson@earthlink.net.
Amnon Dahan and Shachar Ronen, The XLart Group, Inc.;
818-366-8677; fax: 818-832-9211; *e-mail:* info@xlartgroup.com;
website: xlartgroup.com.
PHOTOGRAPHER. Edmund Barr
RESOURCES. *Tiles:* Bussell Tiles; 310-456-9575;
e-mail: janet@busselltiles.com *and* Malibu Tile Works;
310-456-0777; *e-mail:* Malibutileworks@aol.com;
website: malibutileworks.com. *Furniture:* Oasis Furniture;
310-456-9883. *Natural stones:* Modul Marble and Granite;
818-767-4528; *e-mail:* modulmarble@aol.com;
website: modulmarble.com.

PAGES **144–151**, PICTURE PERFECT, EPISODE **821**

DESIGNERS. Richard W. Herb, Richard W. Herb Interiors;
310-278-5033; fax: 310-278-2470; *e-mail:*
rwherb@richardherbinteriors.com.
Michele Stone, Michele Stone Interior Design; 626-799-1174;
website: reaumeconstruction.com.
David Reaume, David Reaume Construction and Design;
626-795-7810; fax: 626-793-1687; *e-mail:* davidbreaume@aol.com;
website: reaumeconstruction.com.
Dan Bissell, Dan Bissell Interior Design; 626-852-7911;
fax: 626-852-7914.
PHOTOGRAPHER. Edmund Barr
RESOURCES. *Tiles:* Mission Tile West Design Studio; 310-434-
9697; *website:* missiontilewest.com. *and* Sonoma Tile Makers;
website: sonomatilemakers.com. *Custom millwork:* Mission
Millworks; 626-441-8509; *e-mail:* Mail@mission-millworks.com.
Fireplace: Temco; 909-657-7311; *website:* temcofireplaces.com.
Bath fixtures: St. Thomas Creations; 619-474-9490;
website: stthomascreations.com. *Faucets:* Harden Industries;
website: harden-fisher.com. *Windows:* Milgard Vinyl Windows;
916-635-0700; *website:* milgard.com.

PAGES **152–161**, A COOK'S KITCHEN, EPISODE **808**

DESIGNERS. Cynthia Piana and Lori Souza, Piana Interiors, Inc.;
661-702-9490; fax: 661-257-7018; *e-mail:*

pianainteriors@pacbell.net.
Jane Brooks, Jane Brooks Interiors; 805-379-0042;
fax: 805-373-5124.
Ilene S. Crouppen, Geometrix; 818-991-4999; fax: 818-991-5615;
e-mail: crouppen@adelphia.net; *website:* ilenecrouppen.com.
PHOTOGRAPHER. Edmund Barr
RESOURCES. *Stone:* Olympus Marble & Granite; 818-982-8832;
Appliances: Viking Range Corporation; 662-455-1200; toll-free:
888-845-4641; *website:* vikingrange.com. *Tile:* Walker Zanger;
310-659-1234; *website:* walkerzanger.com.

PAGES **162–169**, RETREAT TO LUXURY, EPISODE **816**

DESIGNERS. Minh-Lien Cohen, Cdesign, Inc.; 818-783-2134;
fax: 818-784-3174; *e-mail:* minh1lien2@aol.com;
website: cdesignla.com.
Jean Blumin and Caren Rideau, Kitchen Design Group;
310-454-6447; fax: 310-459-0928;
e-mail: info@kitchendesigngroup.com;
website: kitchendesigngroup.com.
Mary Broerman, MDB Design Group; 626-296-9160;
fax: 626-296-0460; *e-mail:* mdbdesign@earthlink.net.
PHOTOGRAPHER. Edmund Barr
RESOURCES. *Tile:* Ann Sacks Tile & Stone Inc.; toll-free:
800-278-8453; *website:* annsacks.com. *Electronics:* Sharp USA,
website: sharpusa.com. *Kitchen and bath fixtures:* Kohler;
toll-free: 800-456-4537; *e-mail:* info@kohler.com; *website:*
kohler.com. *Decorative project materials:* Sussman Lifestyle Group;
website: sussmanlifestylegroup.com.

index

to some, inspiration comes naturally.
for the rest of us, may we suggest a good book?

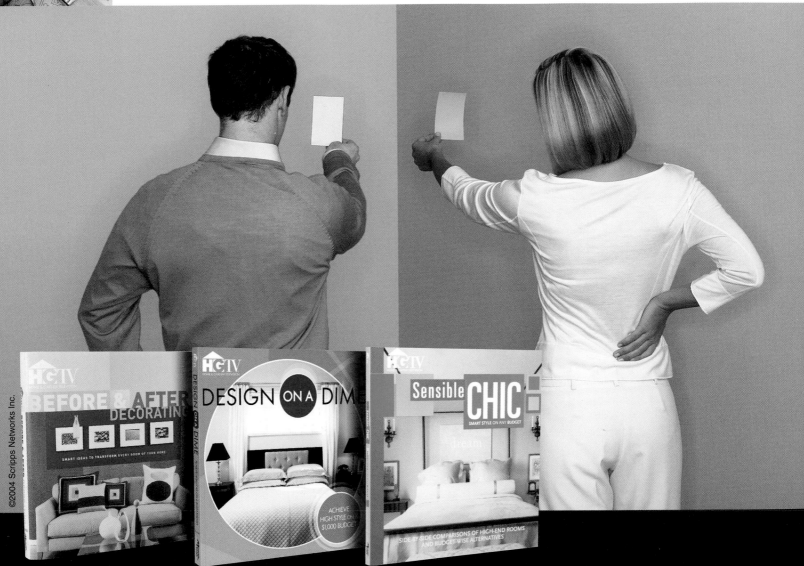

©2004 Scripps Networks Inc.

Make that three good books. In all three, including the popular *Before & After Decorating* and *Design on a Dime,* you'll find simple and affordable design ideas, not to mention plenty of inspiration from HGTV's expert designers. The newest addition, *Sensible Chic,* uses side-by-side comparisons to show how you can imitate a high-end room on a bargain budget.

YOU SHOULD SEE WHAT'S ON !
HGTV.com